This Book Belonges To

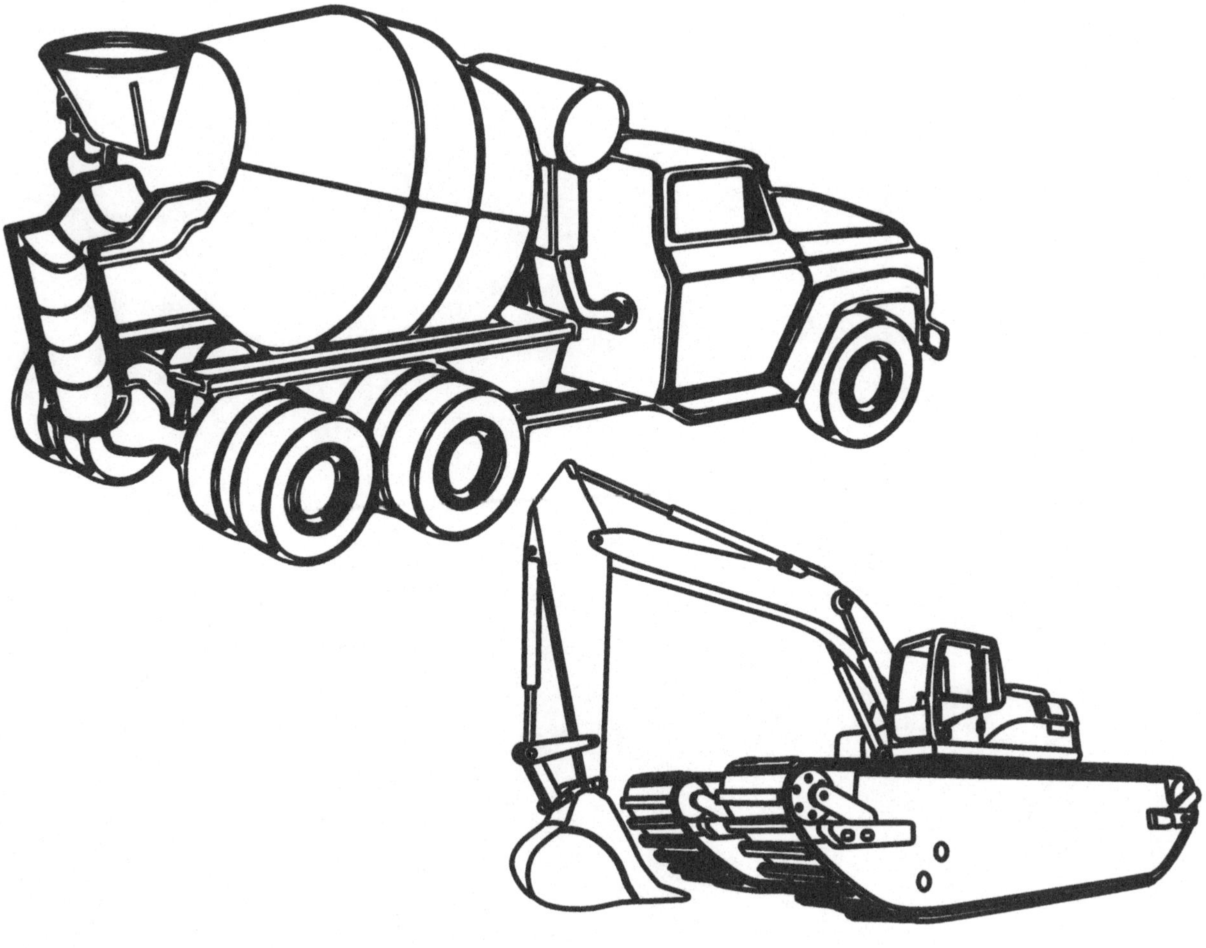

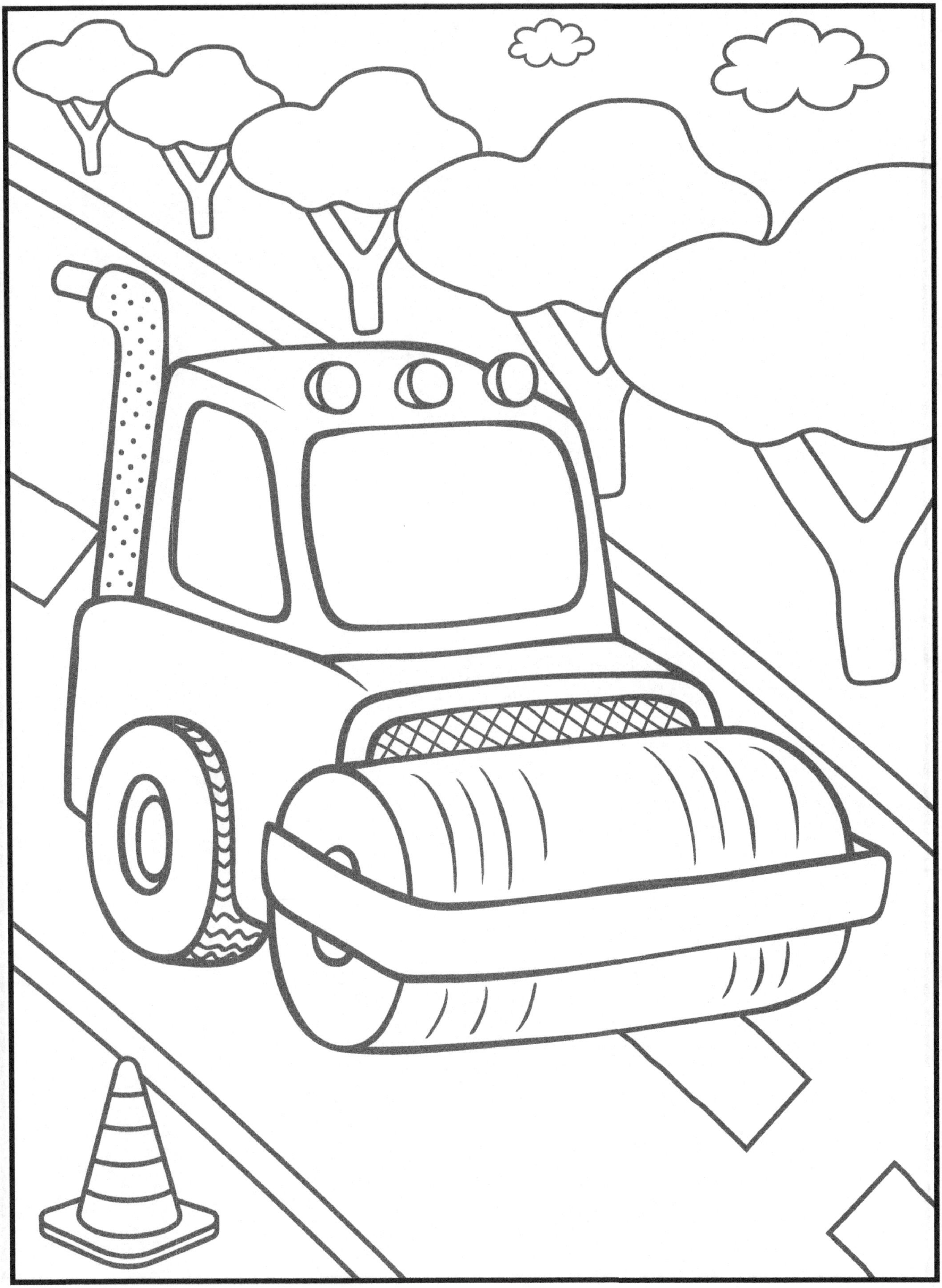

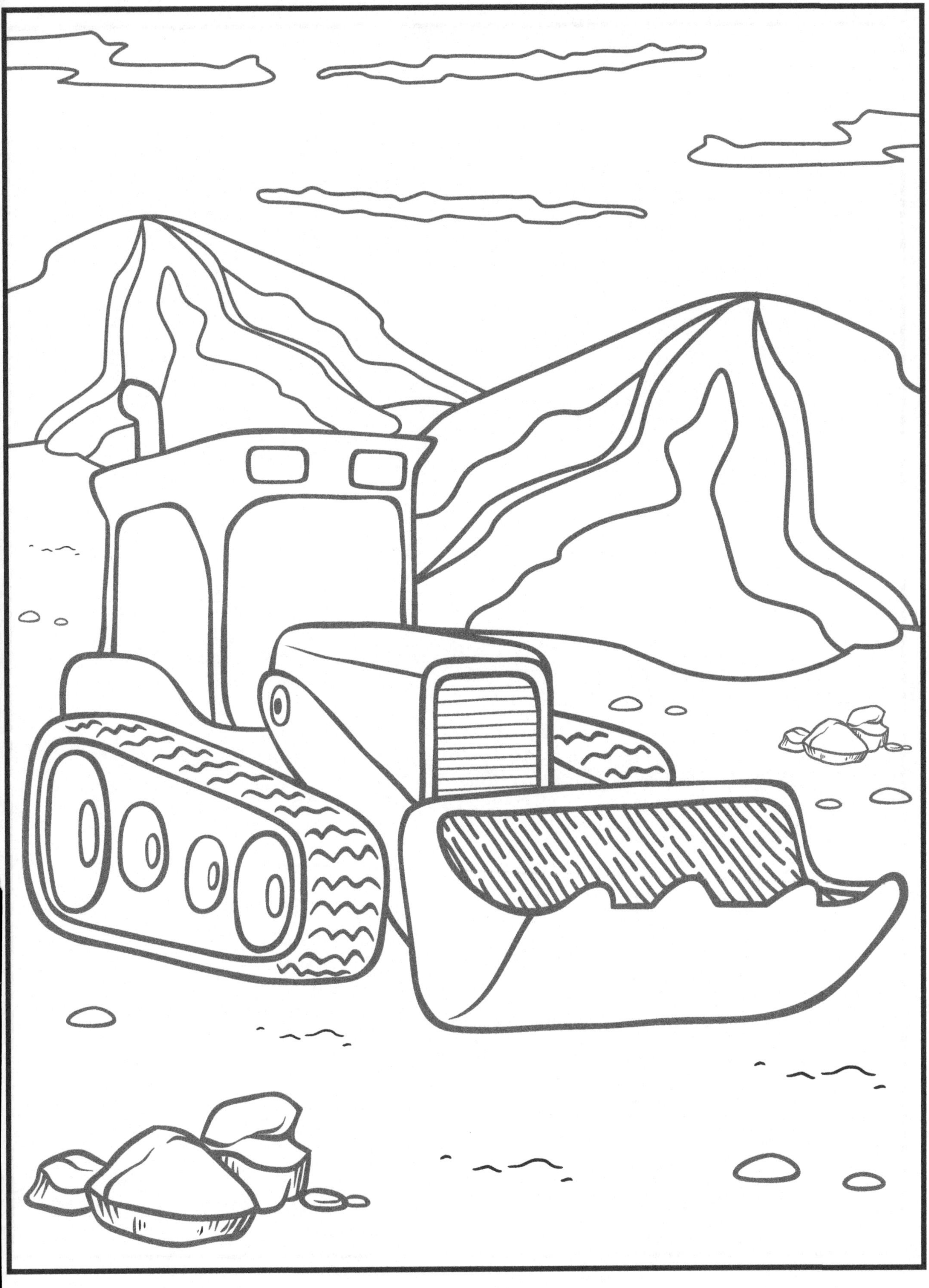

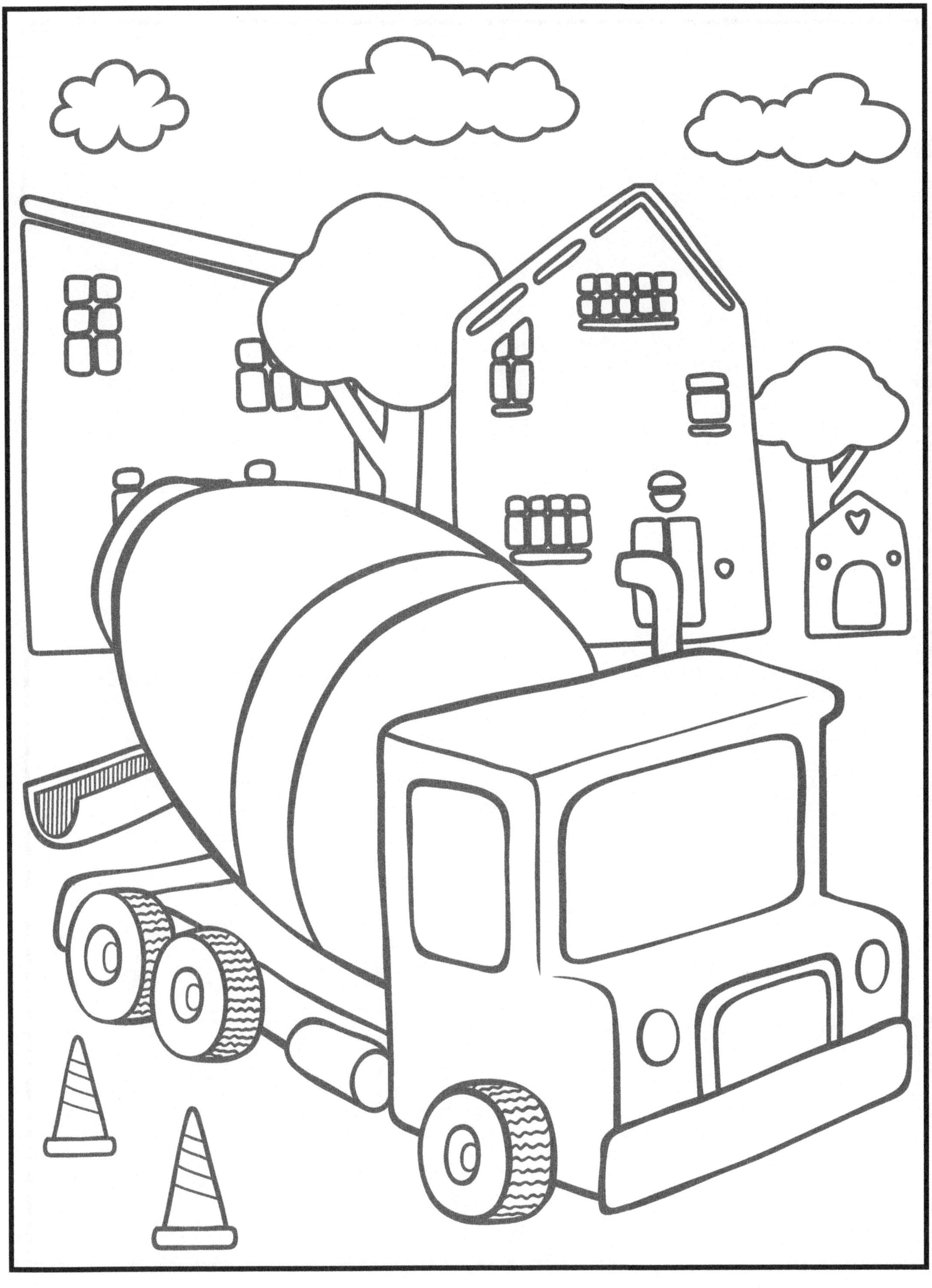

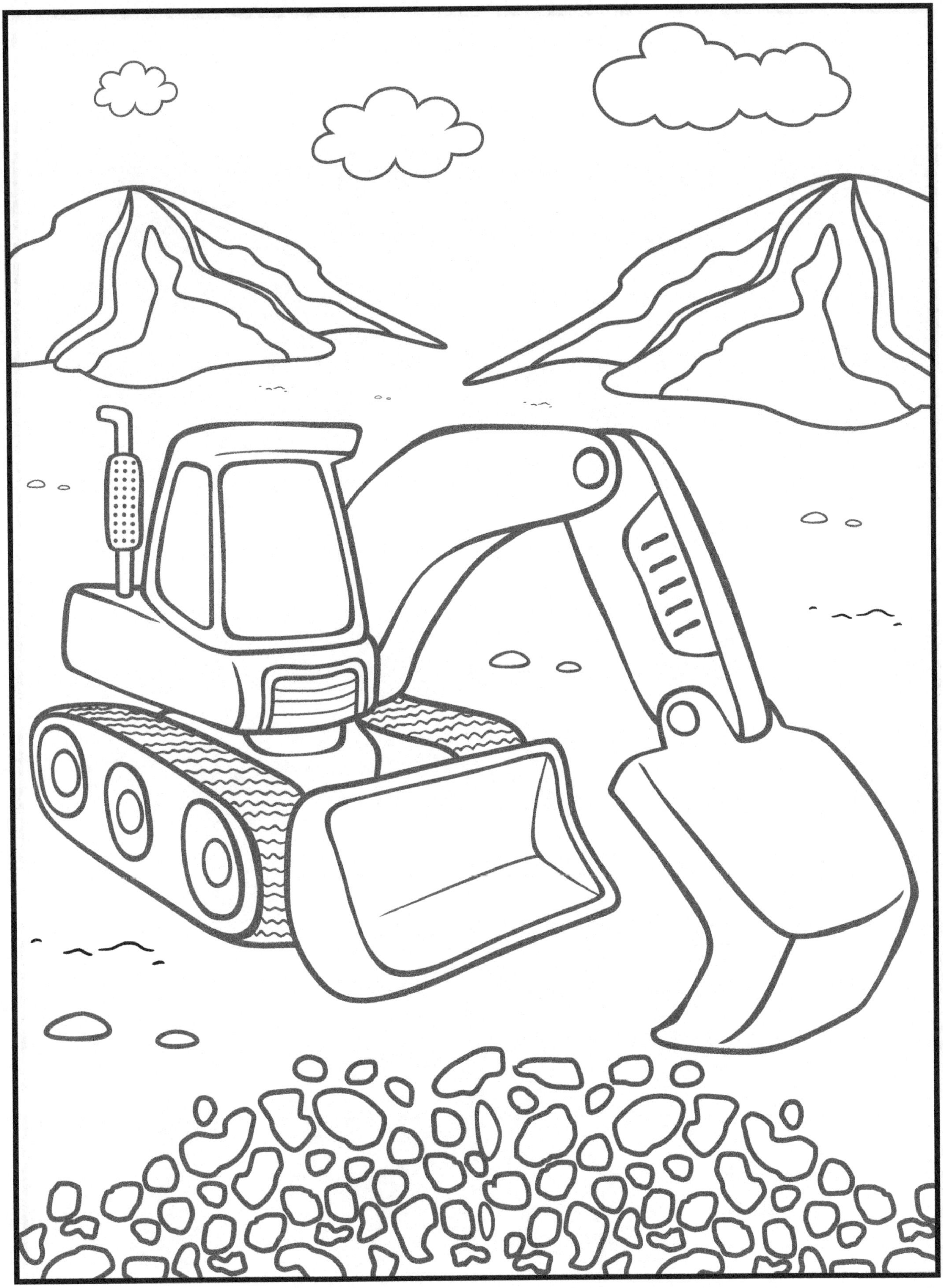

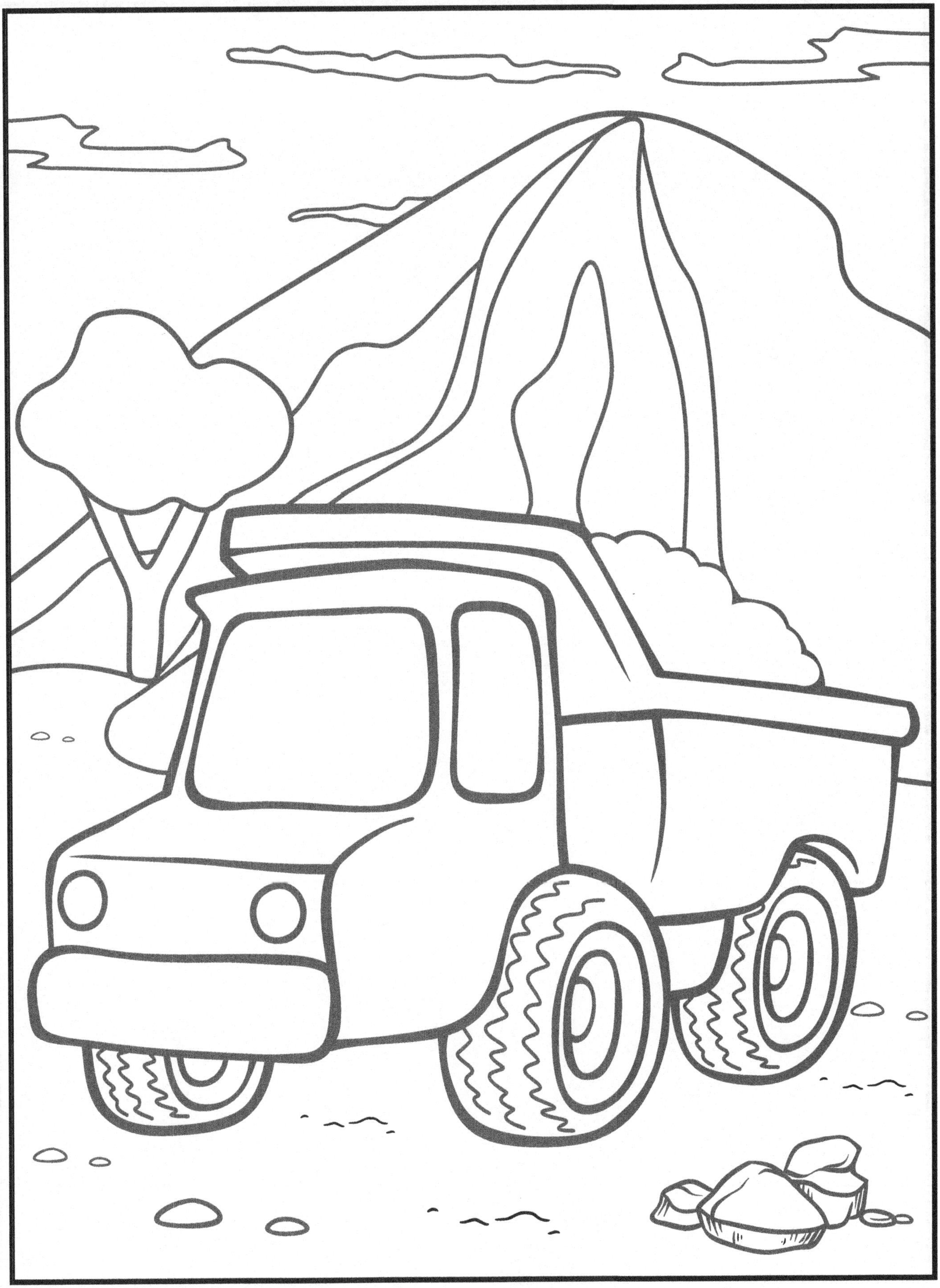

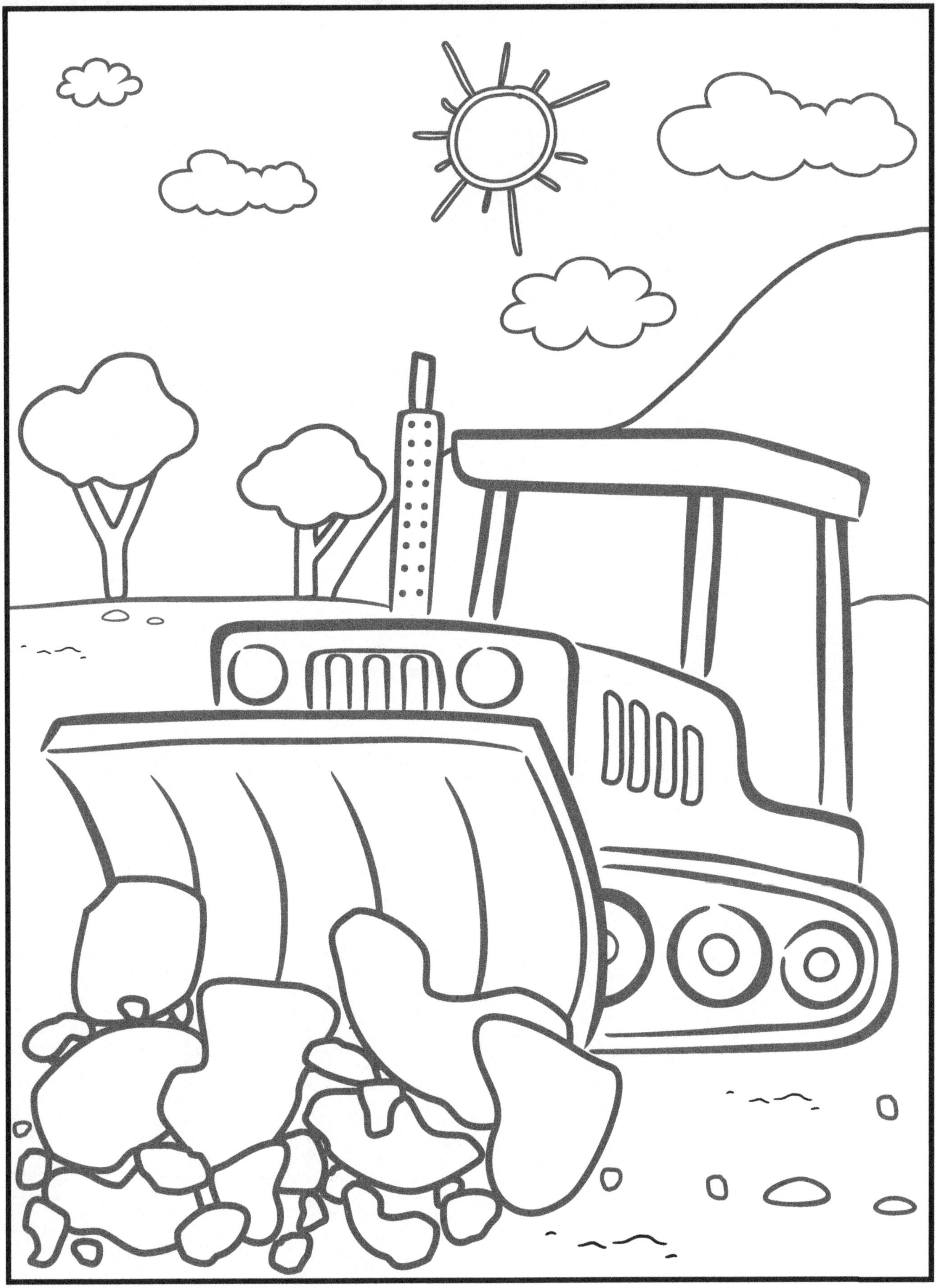

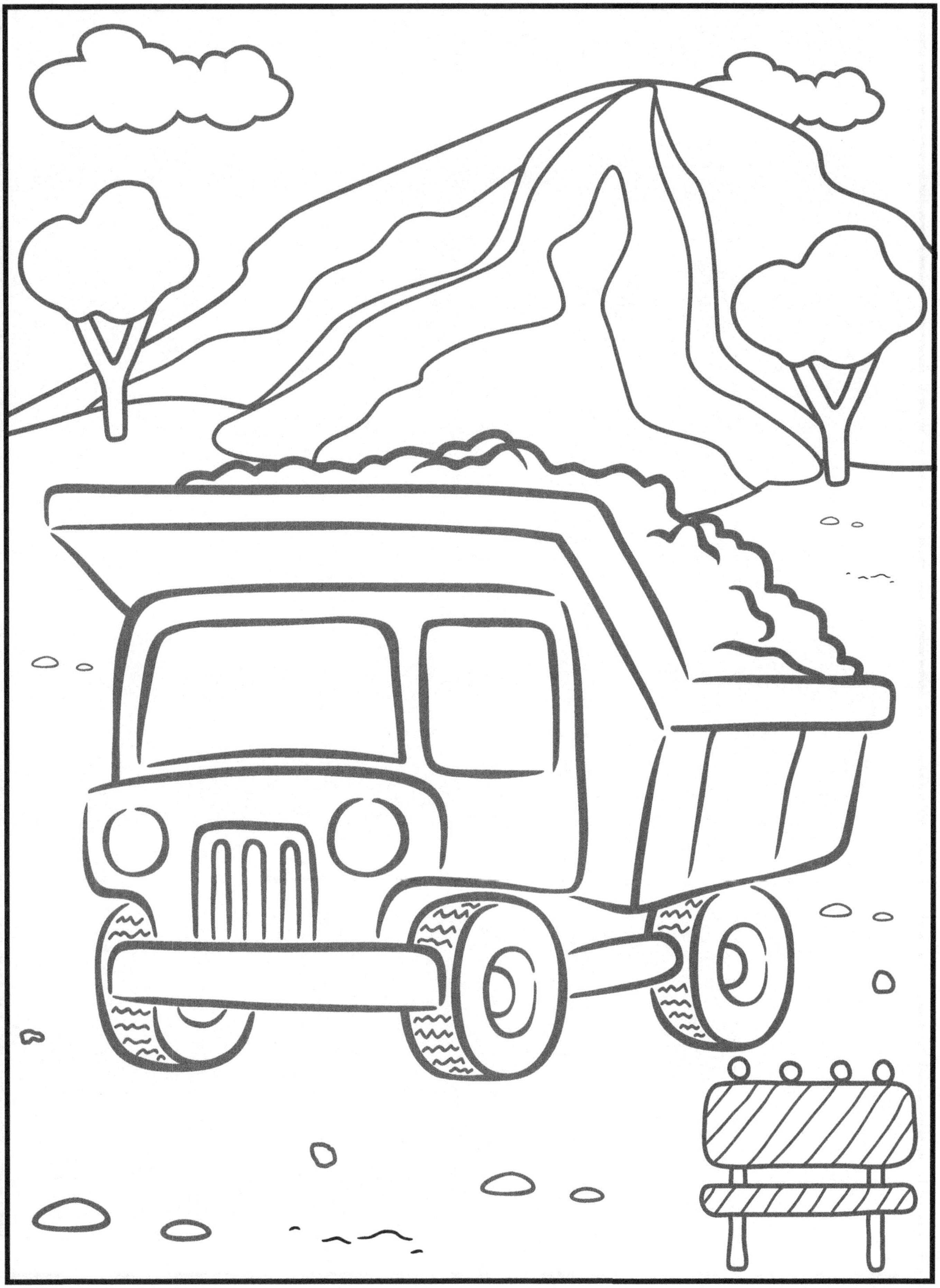

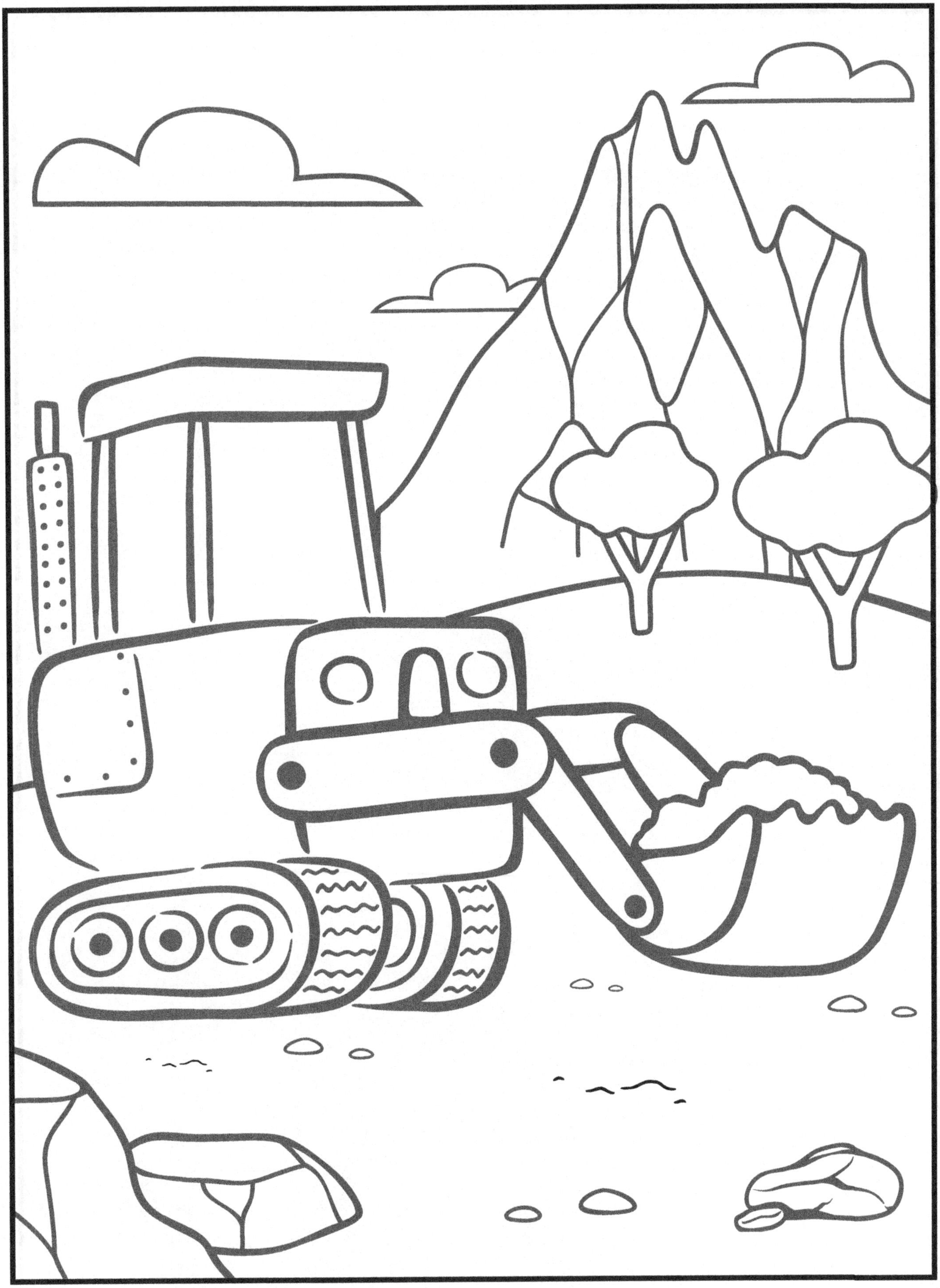

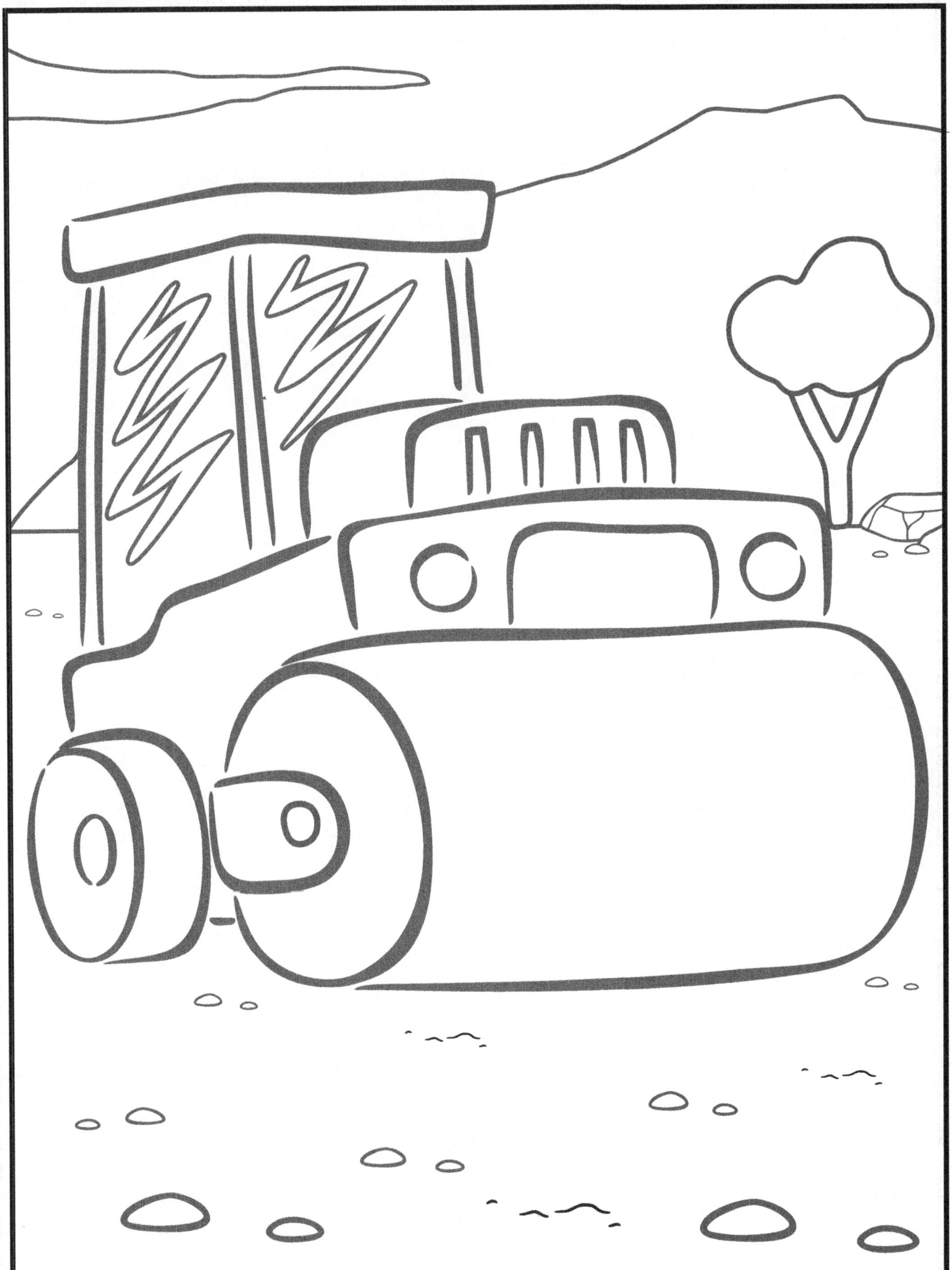

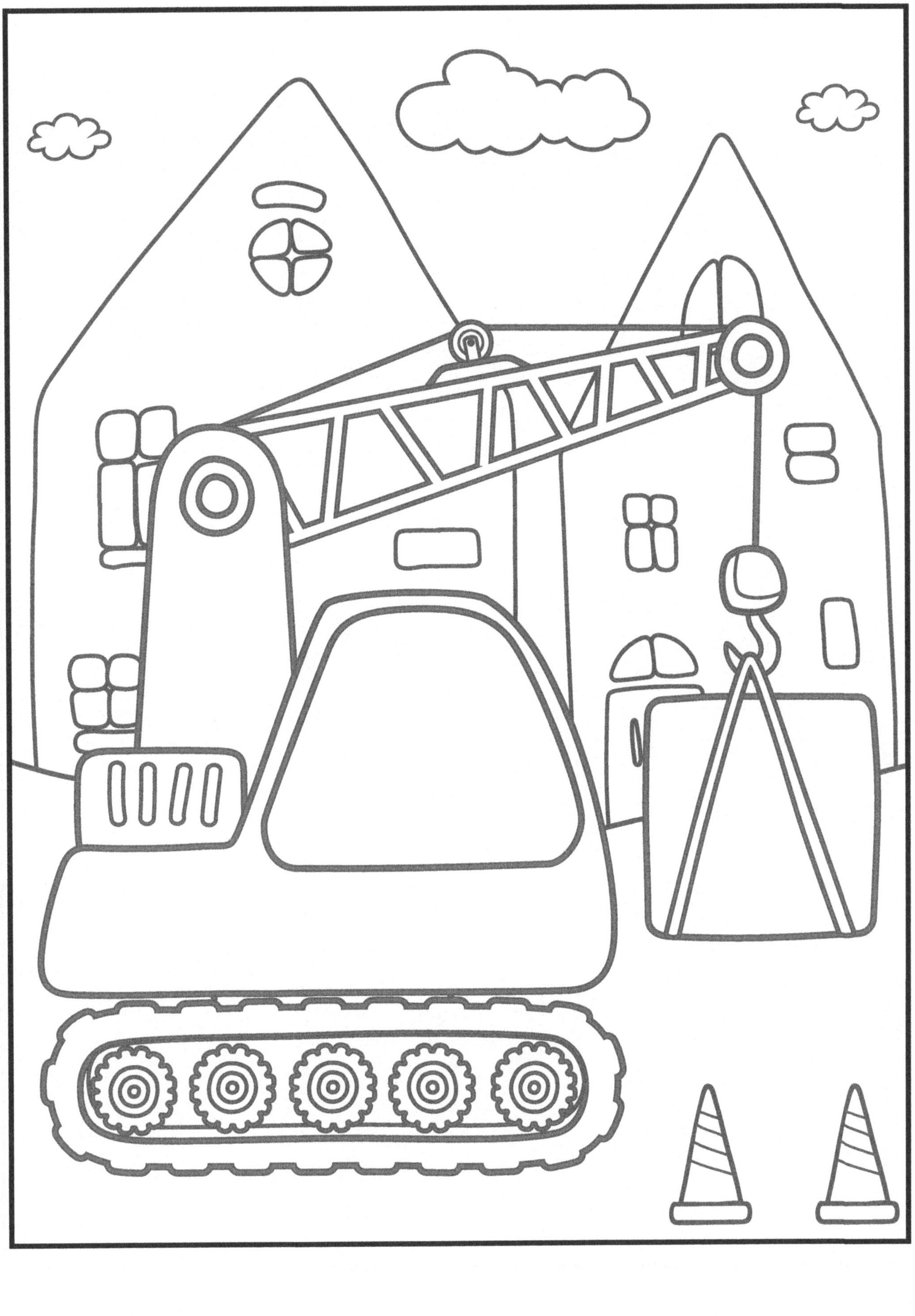

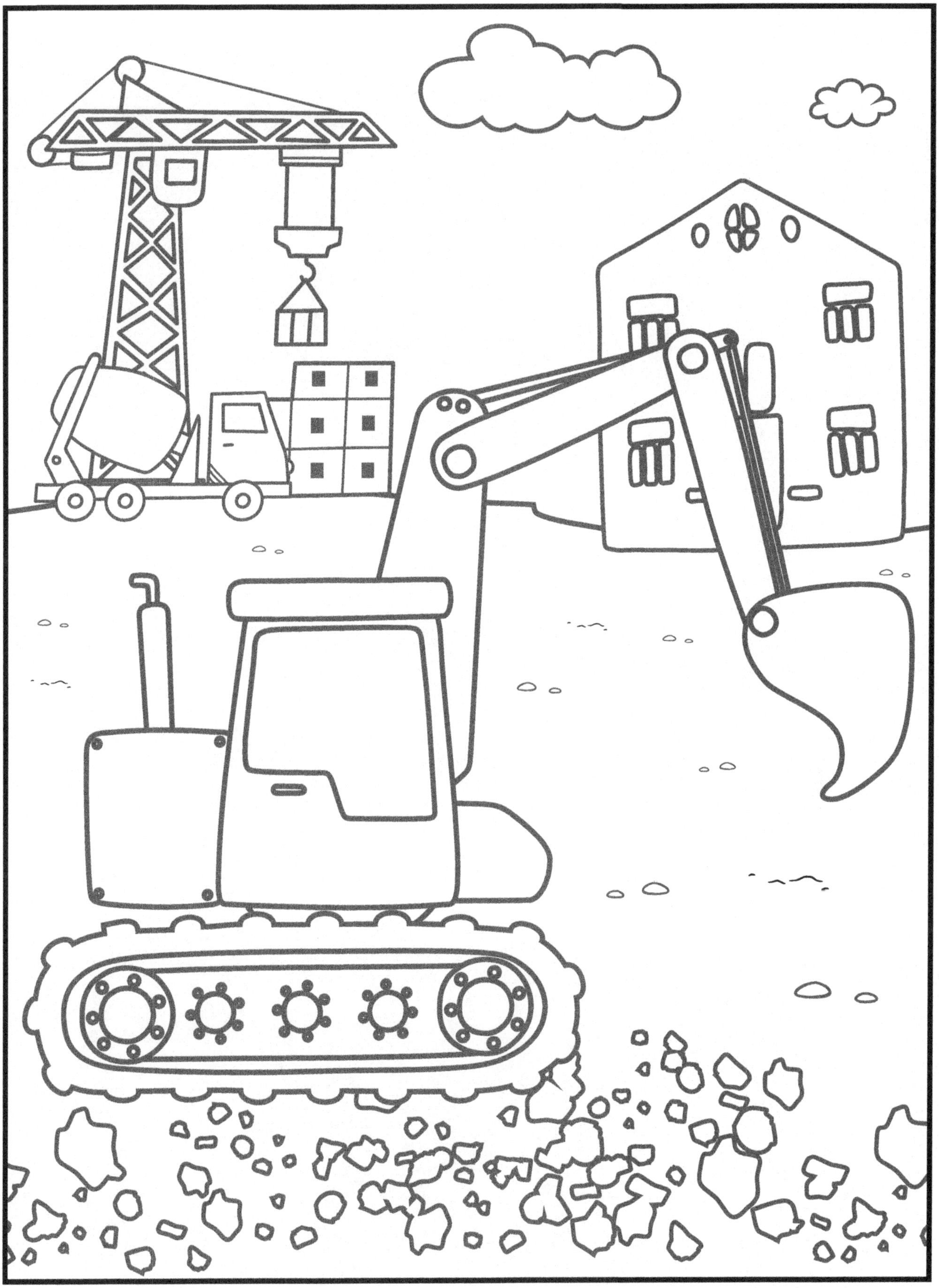

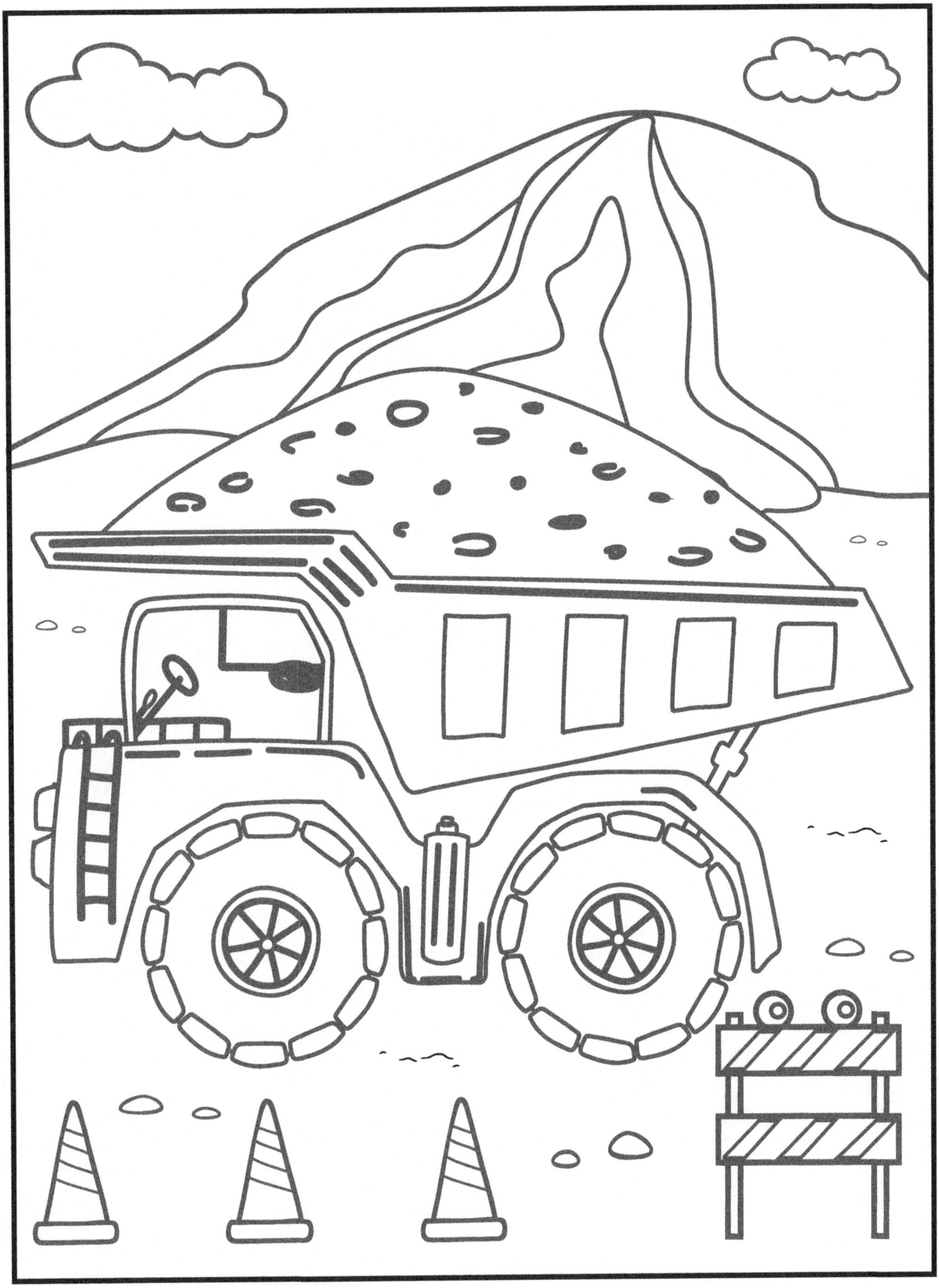

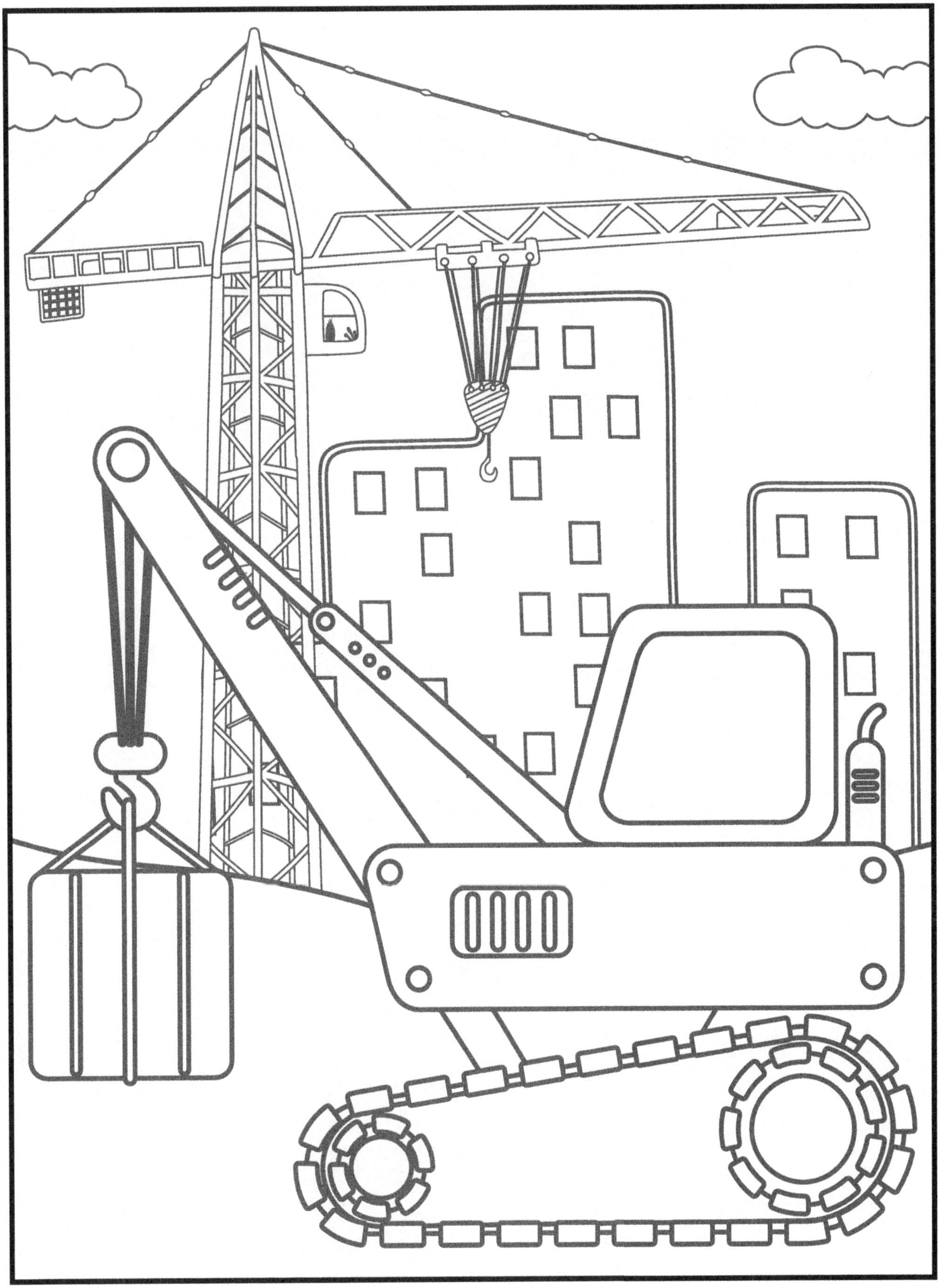

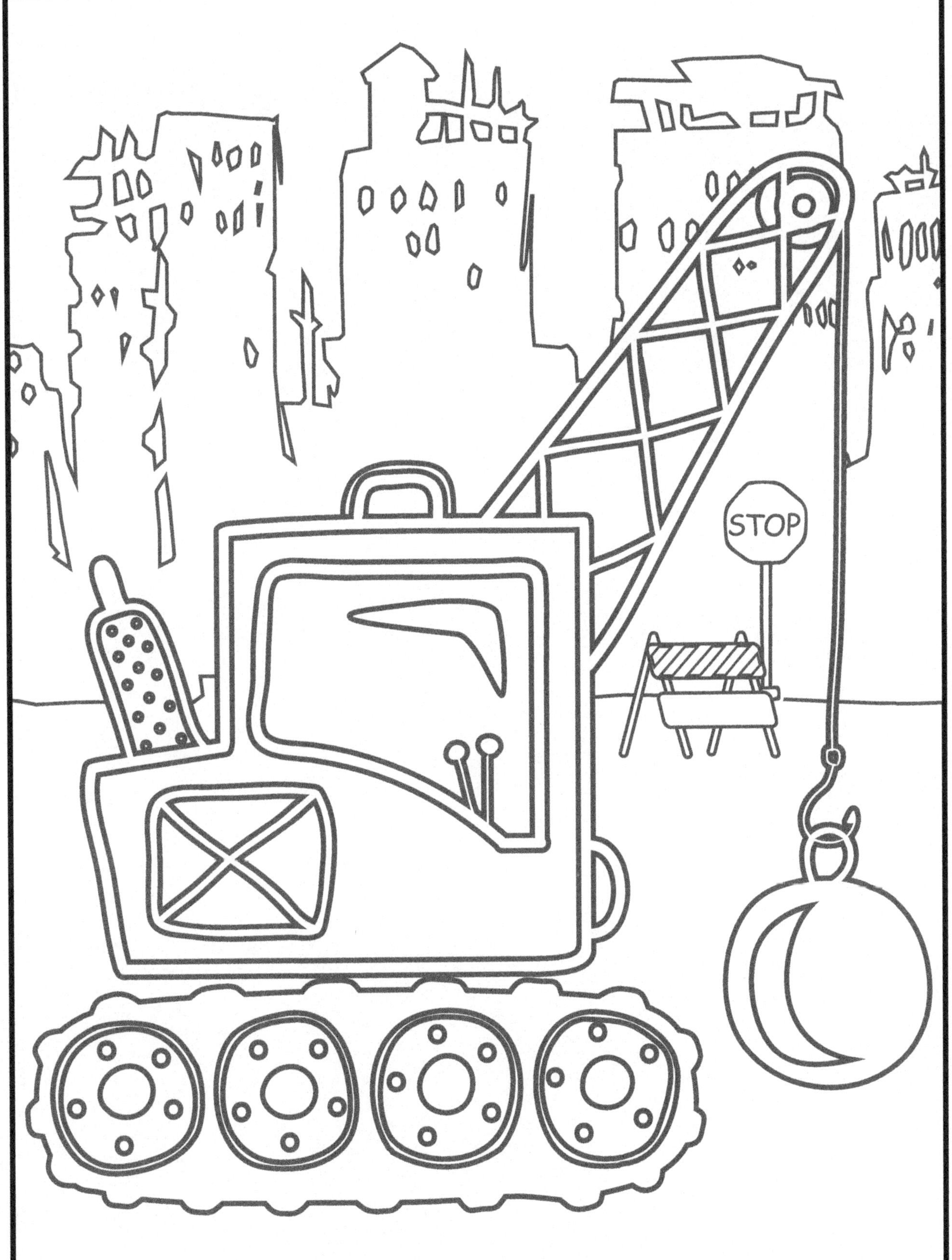
STOP

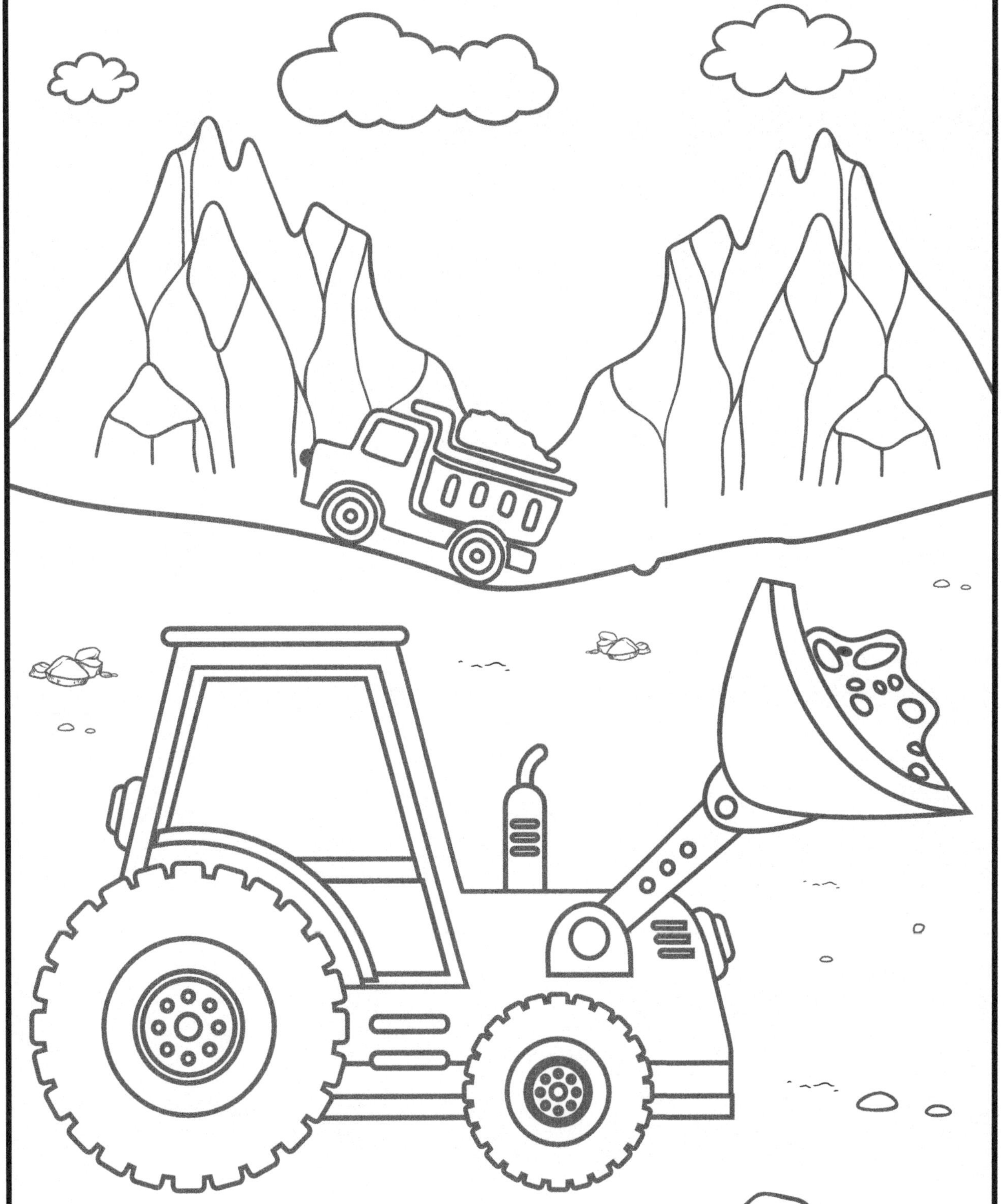

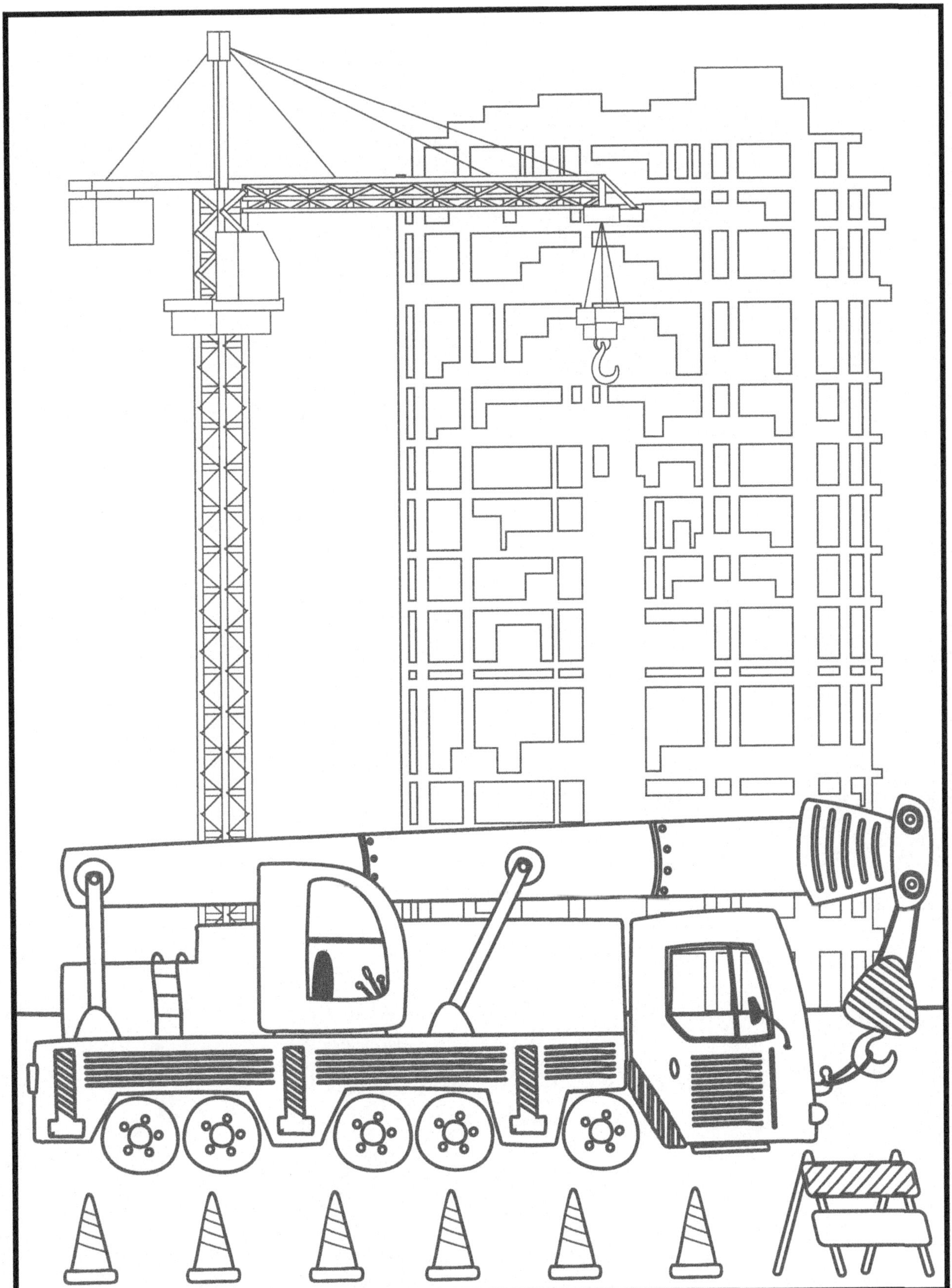

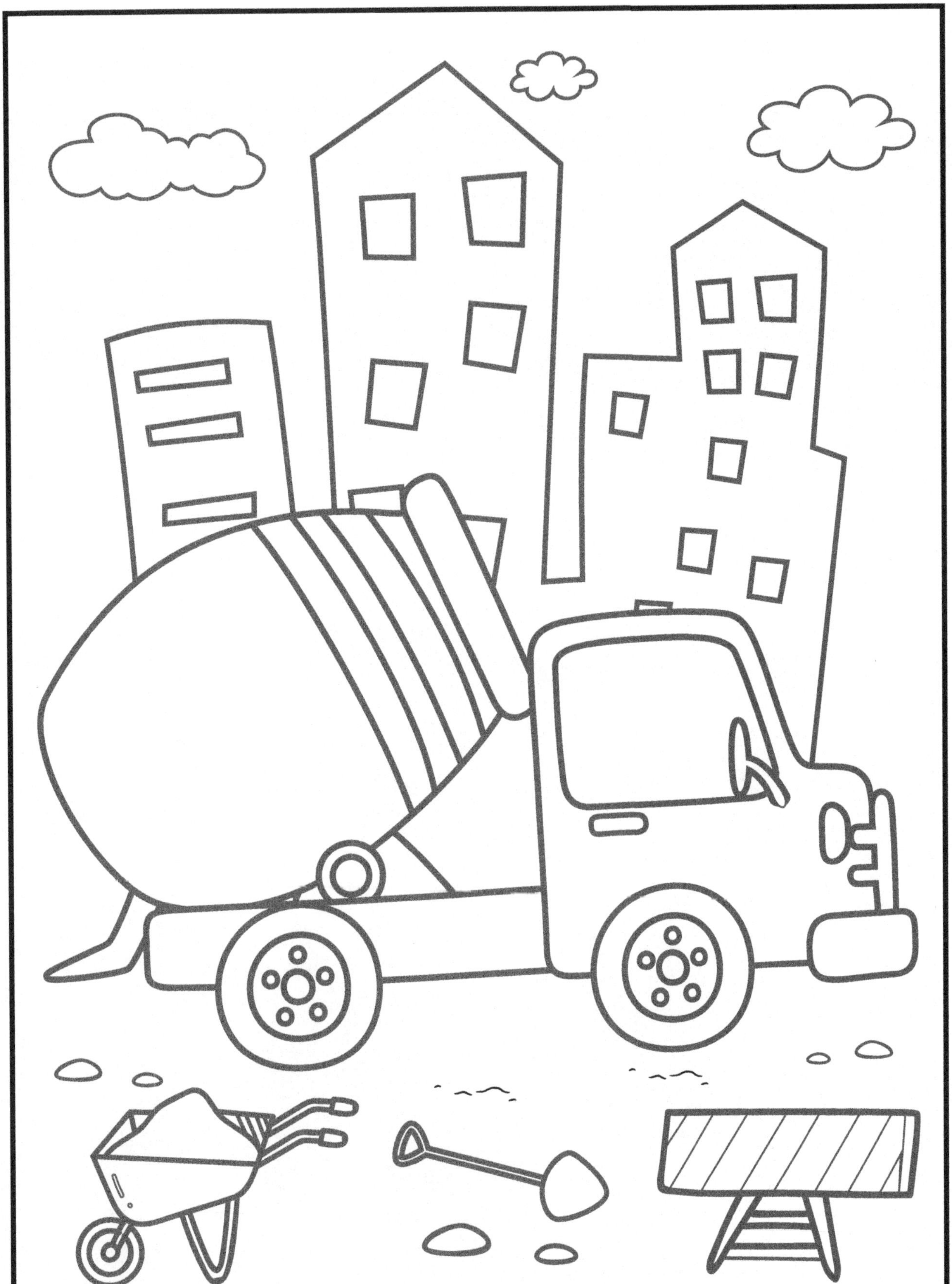

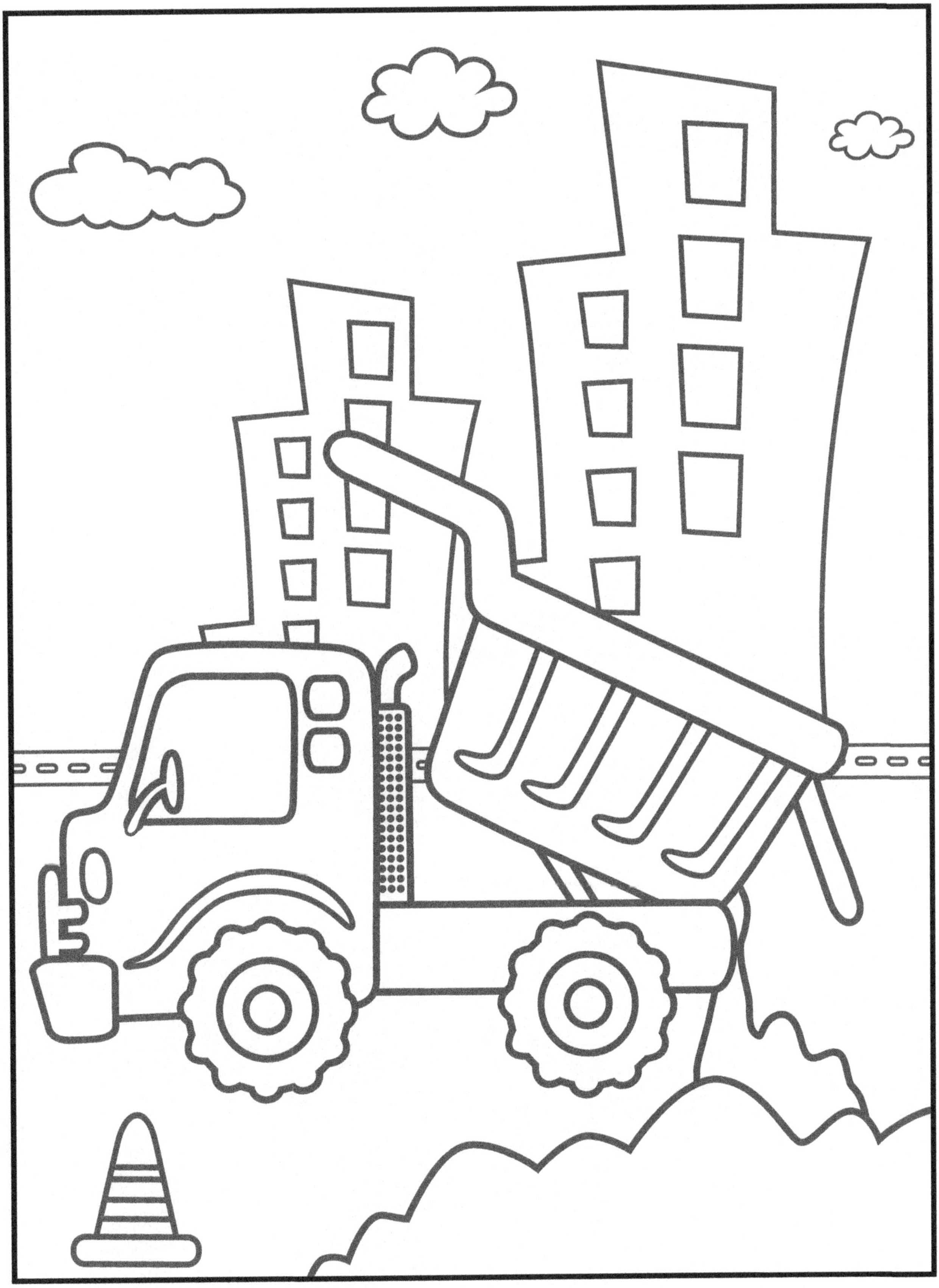

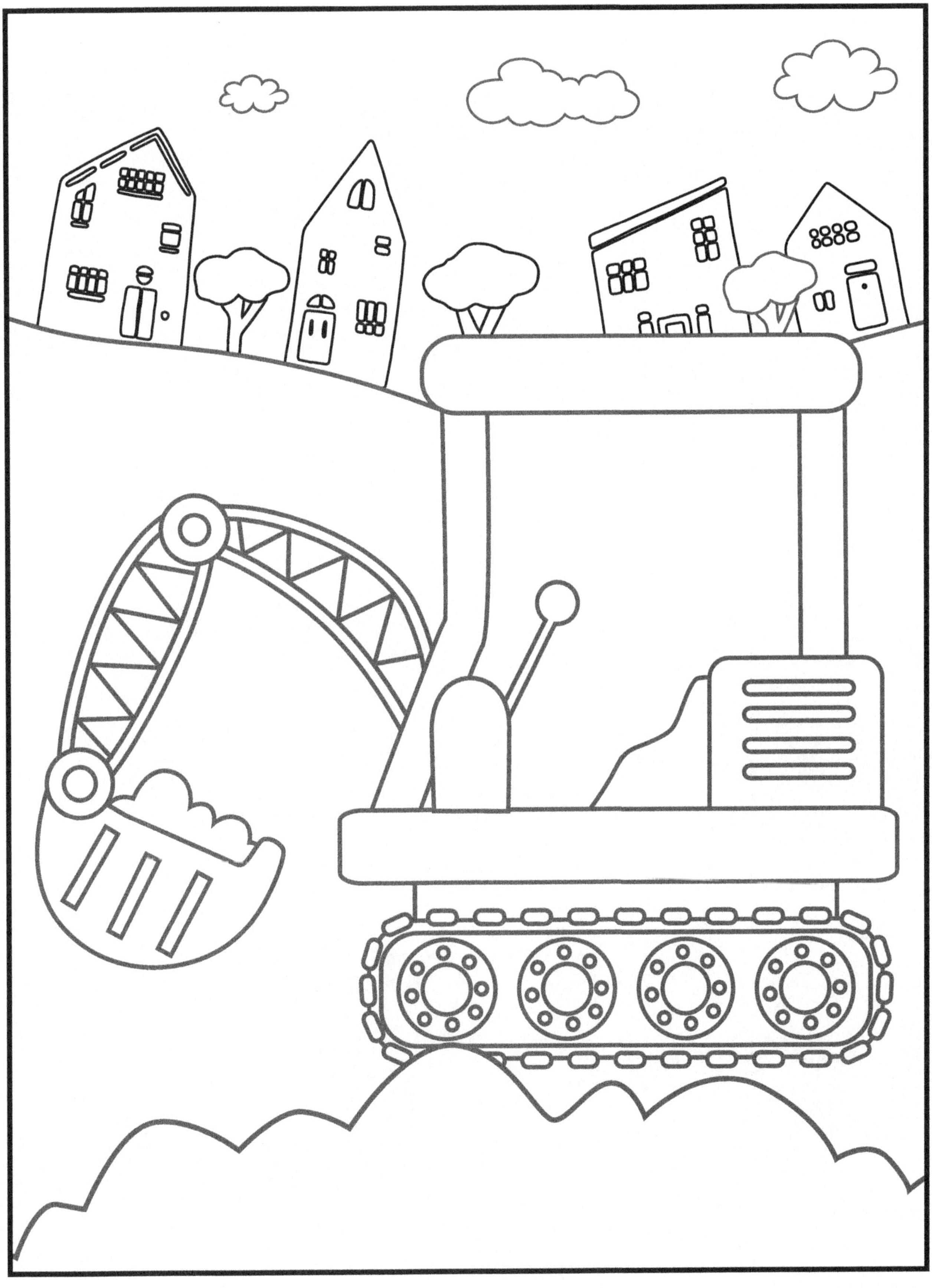

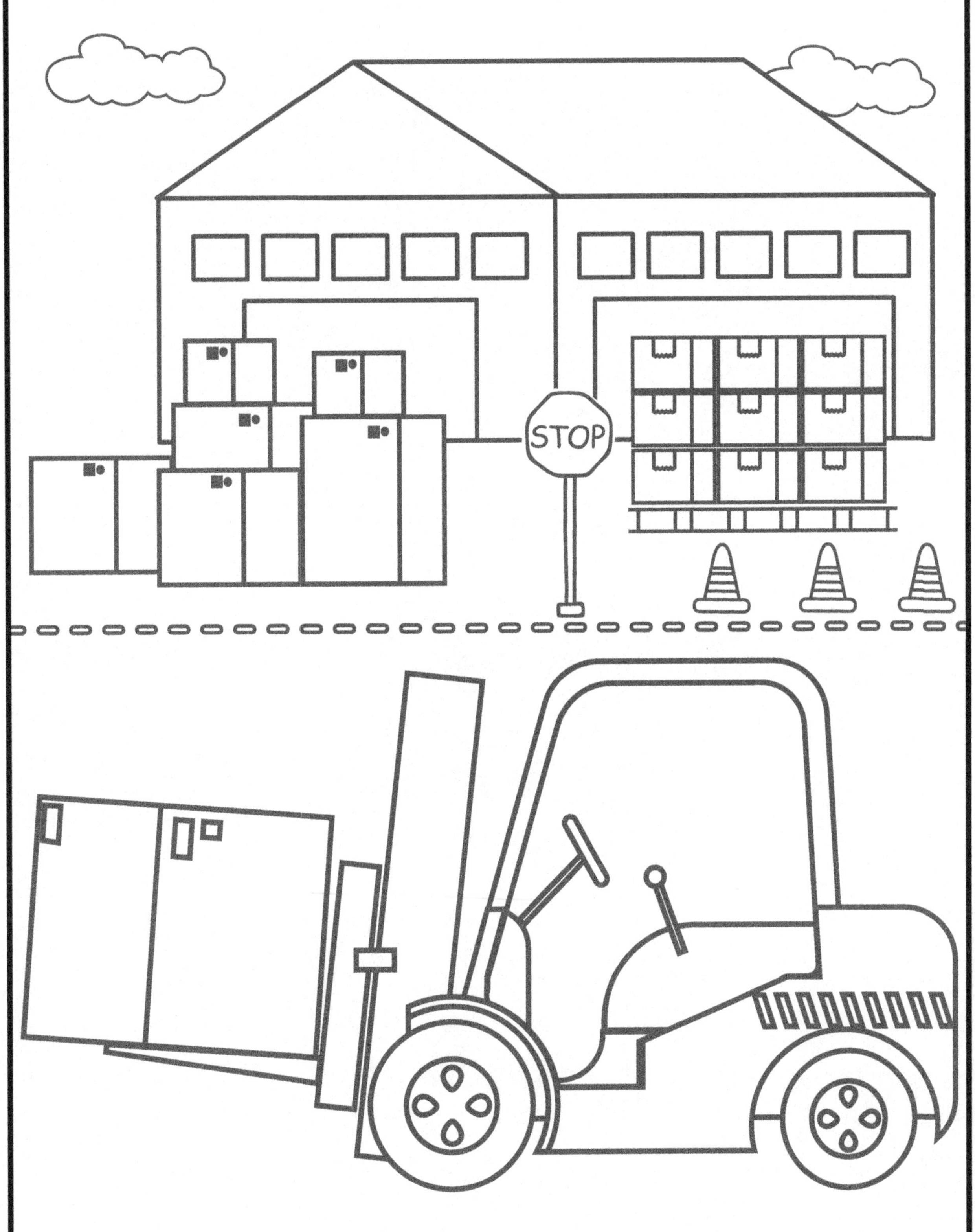
STOP

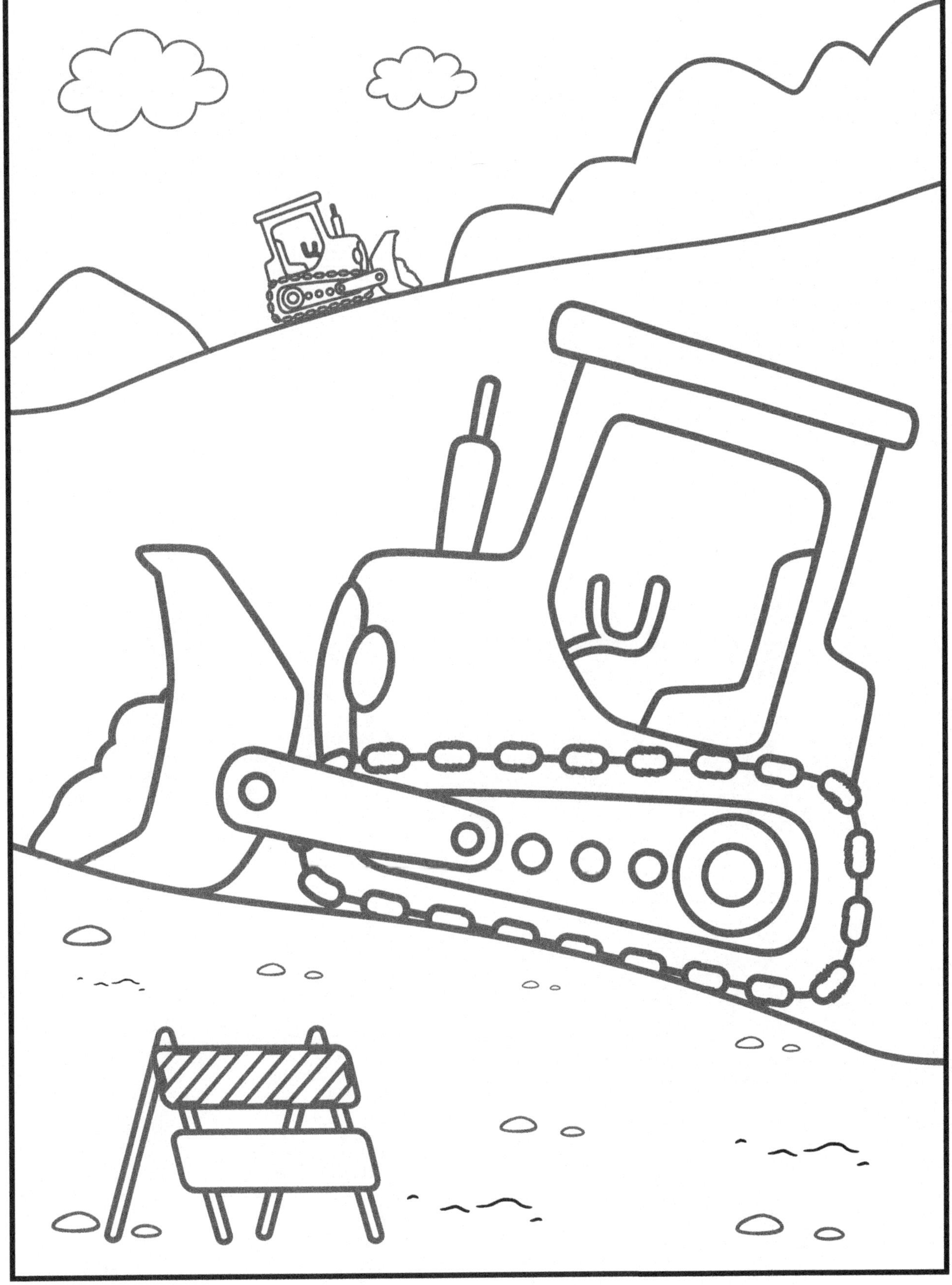

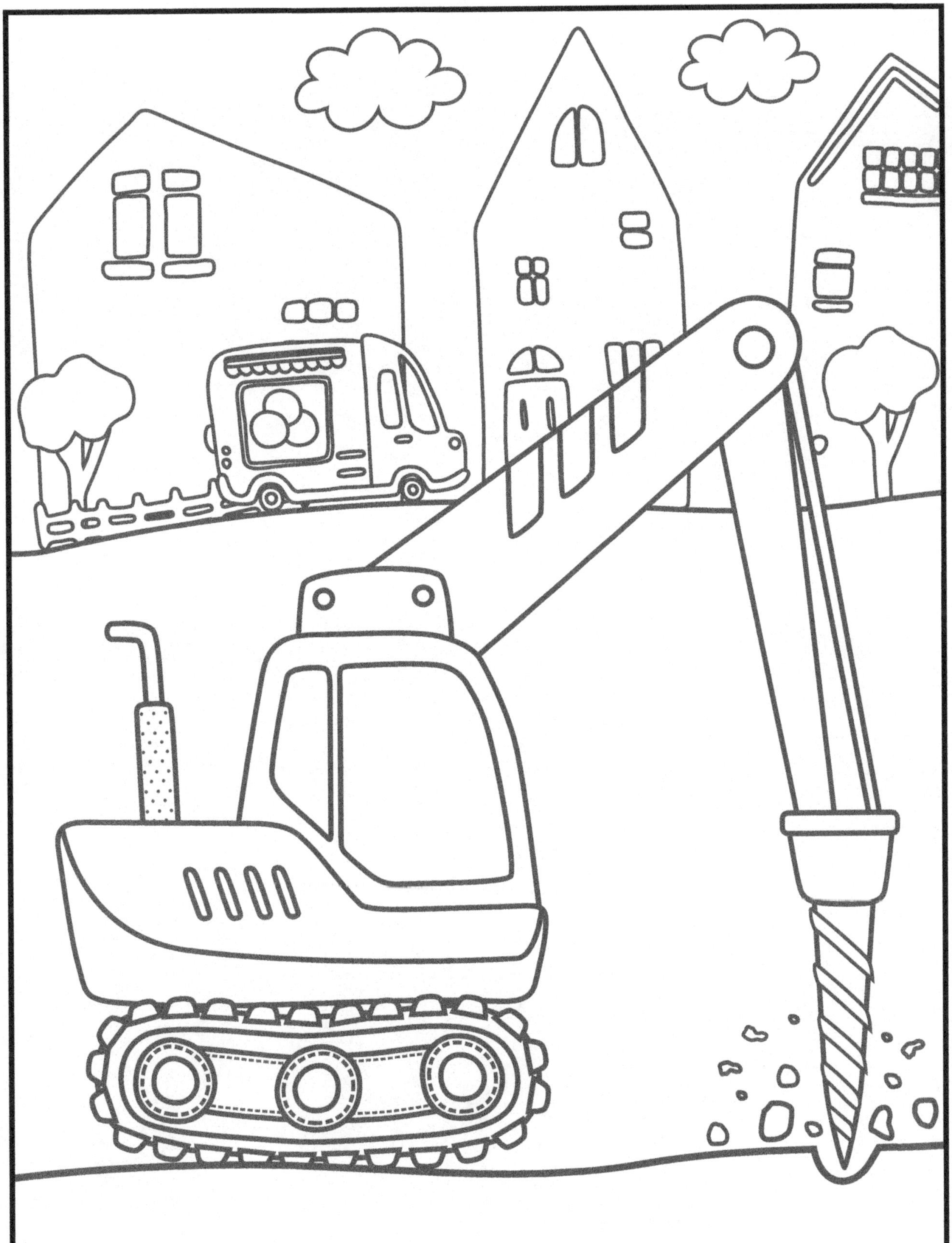

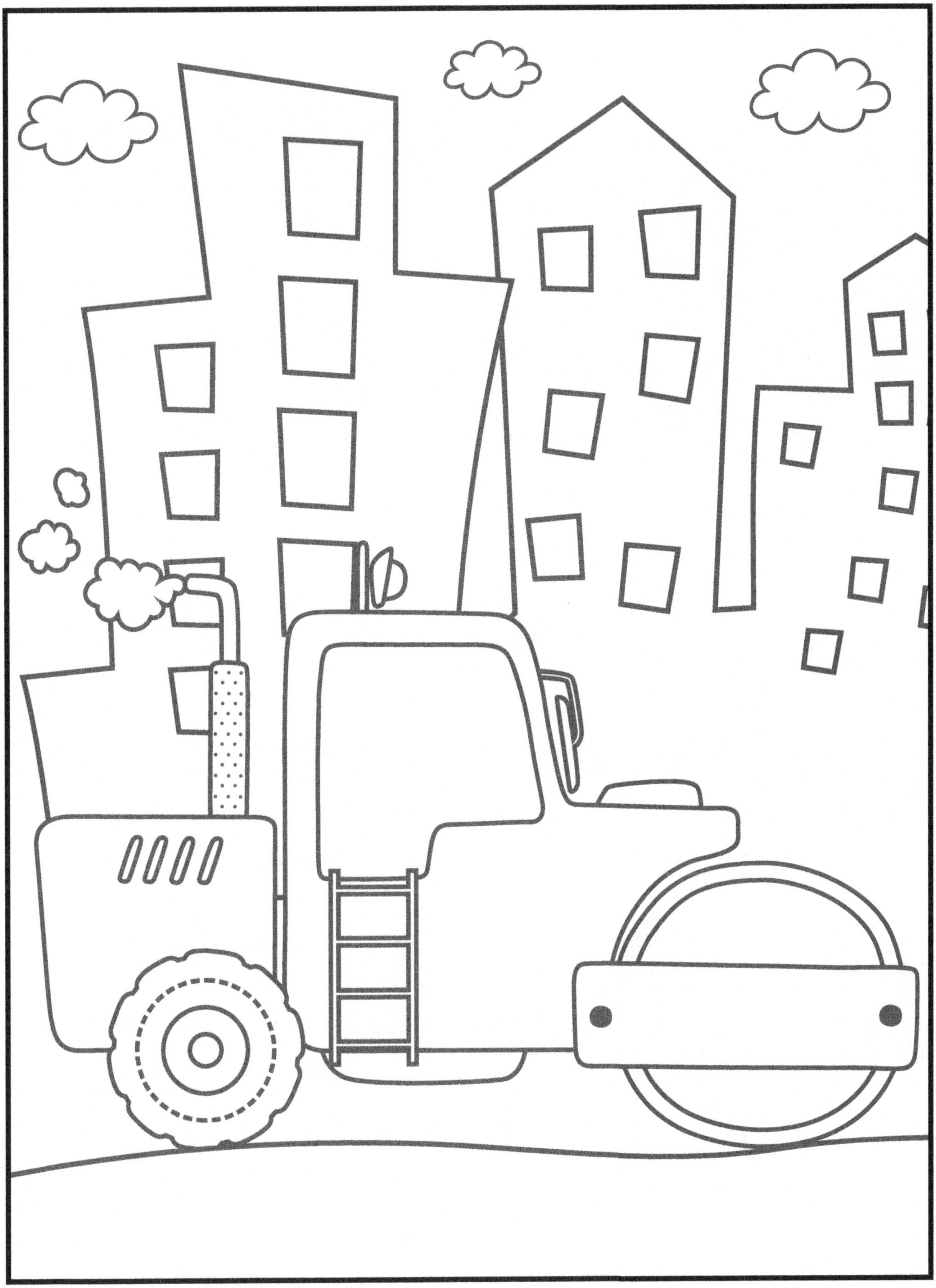

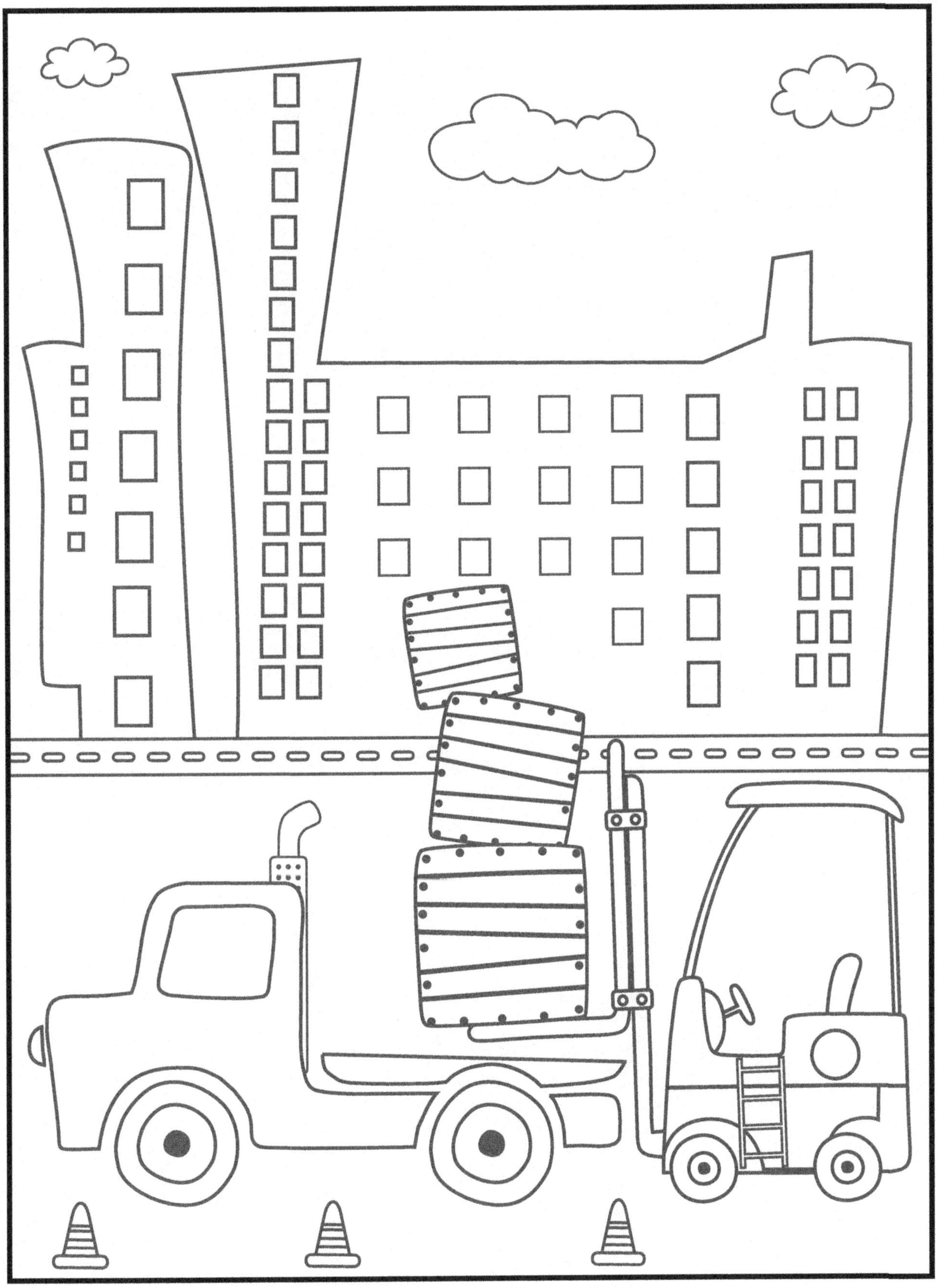

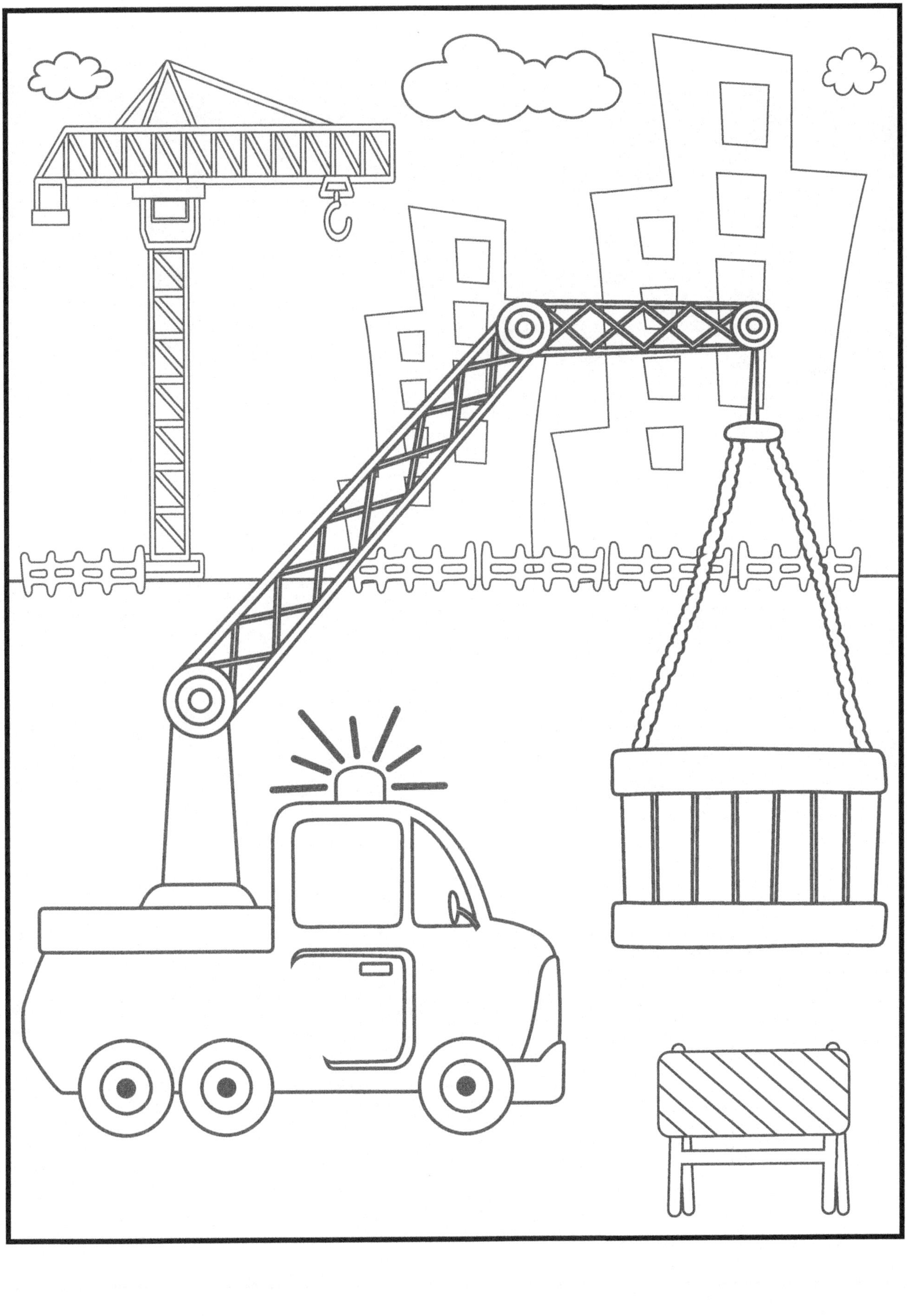

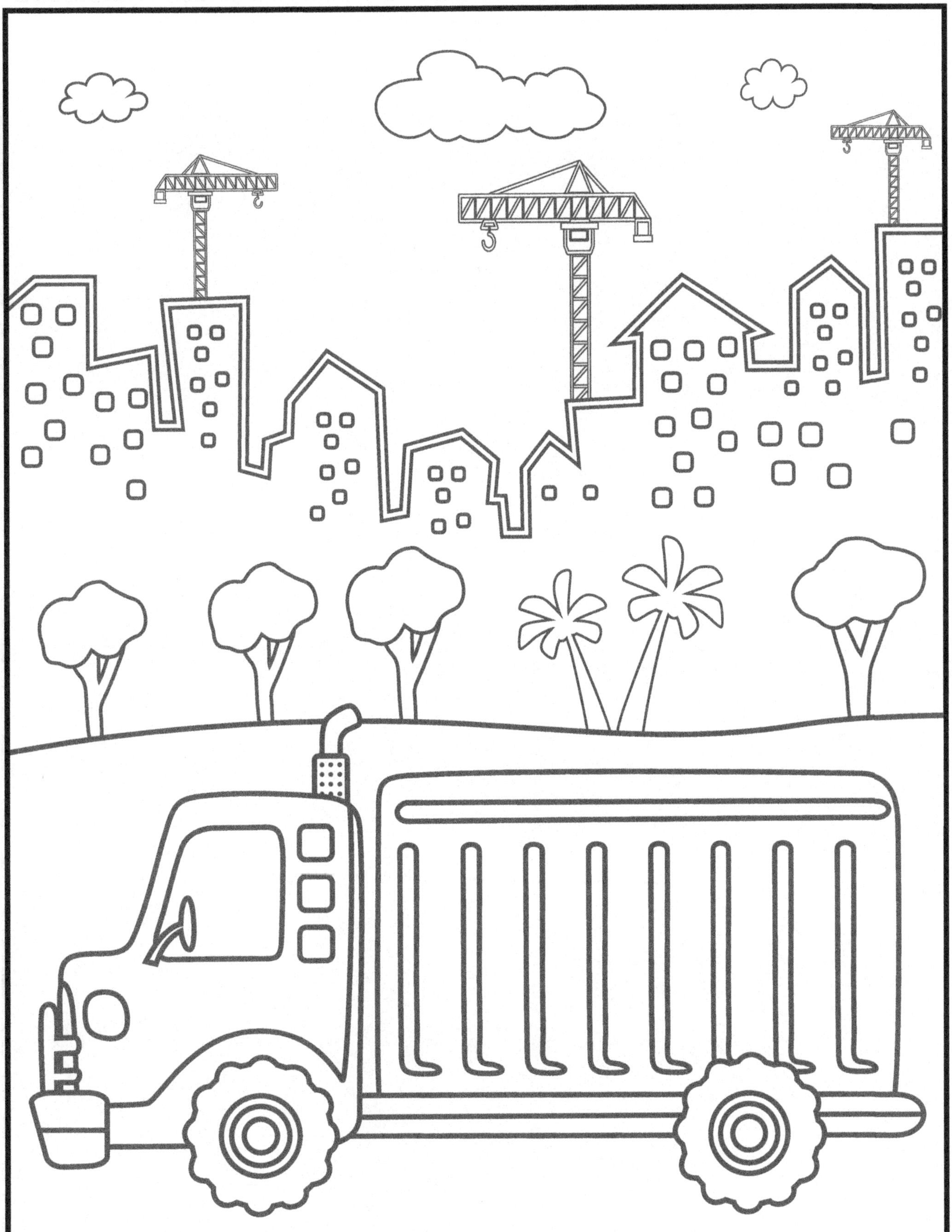

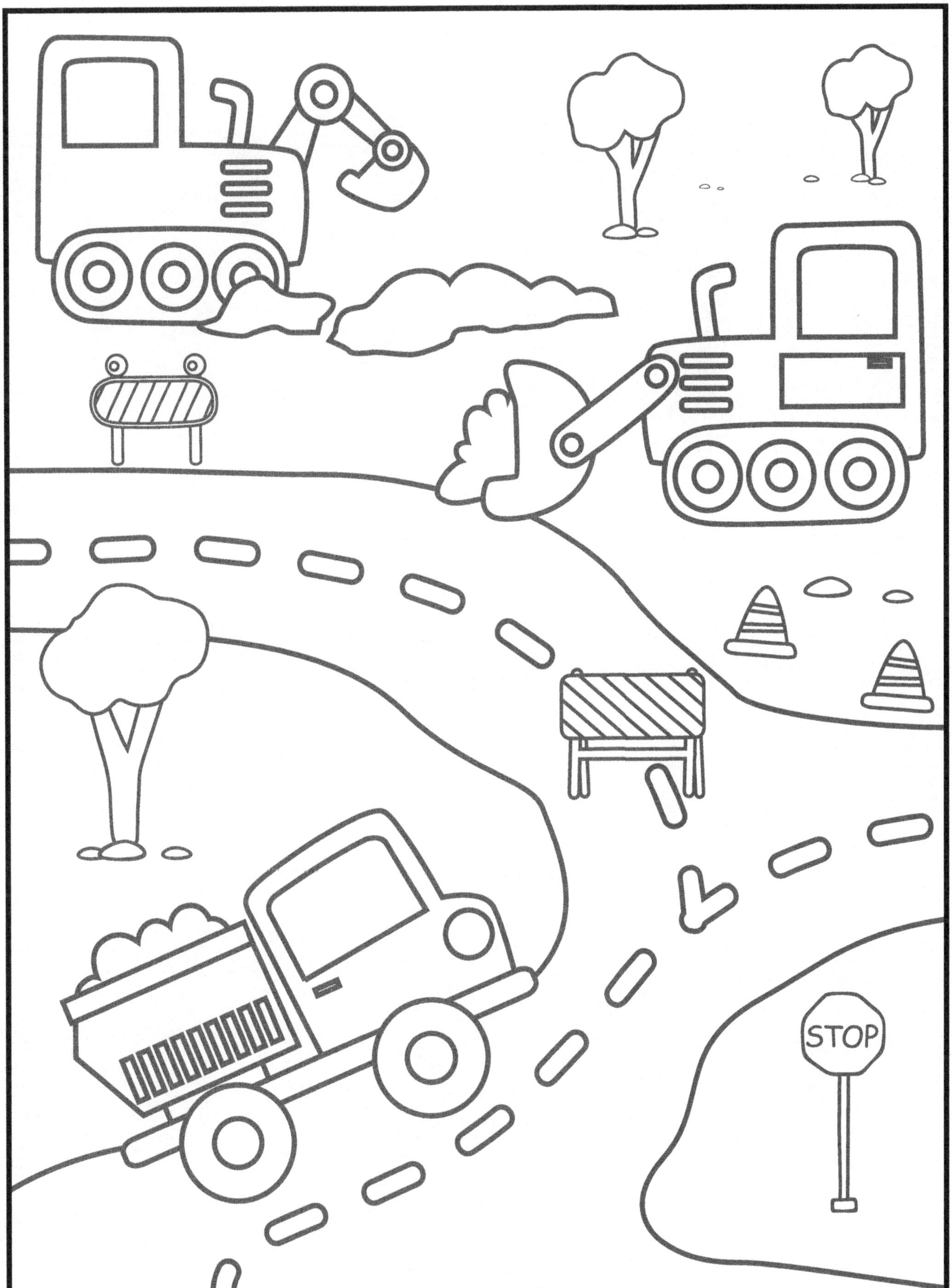
STOP

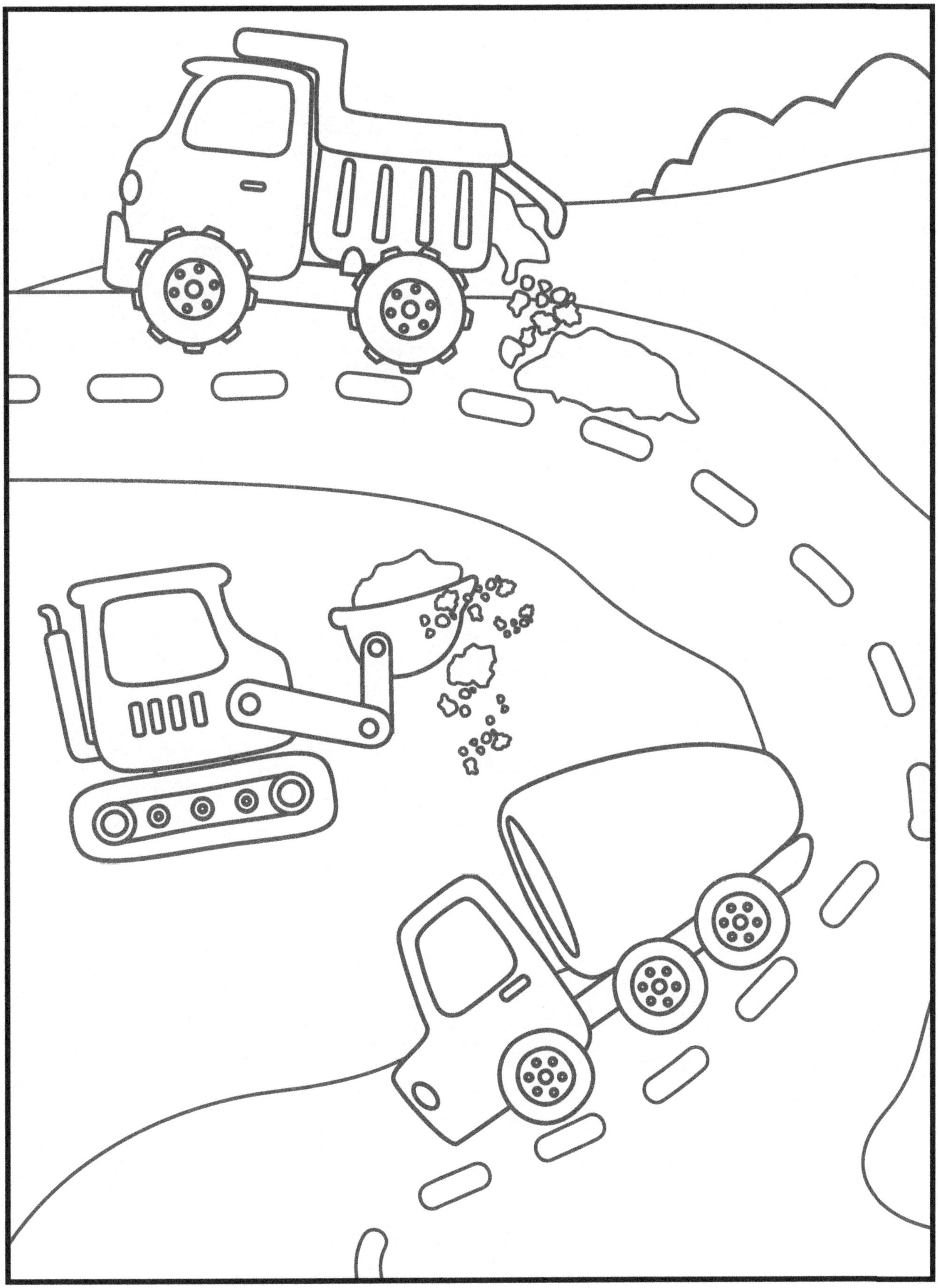

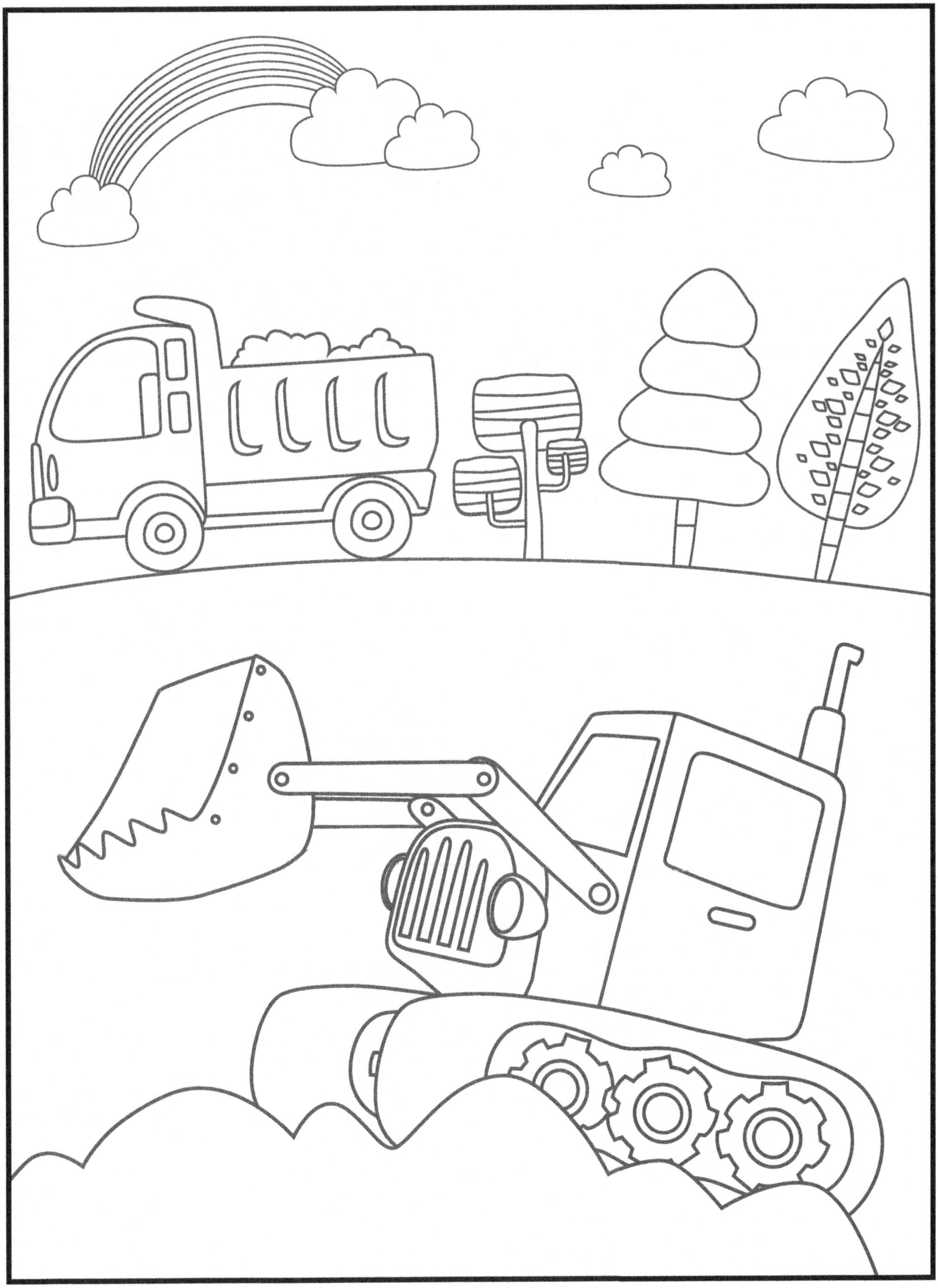

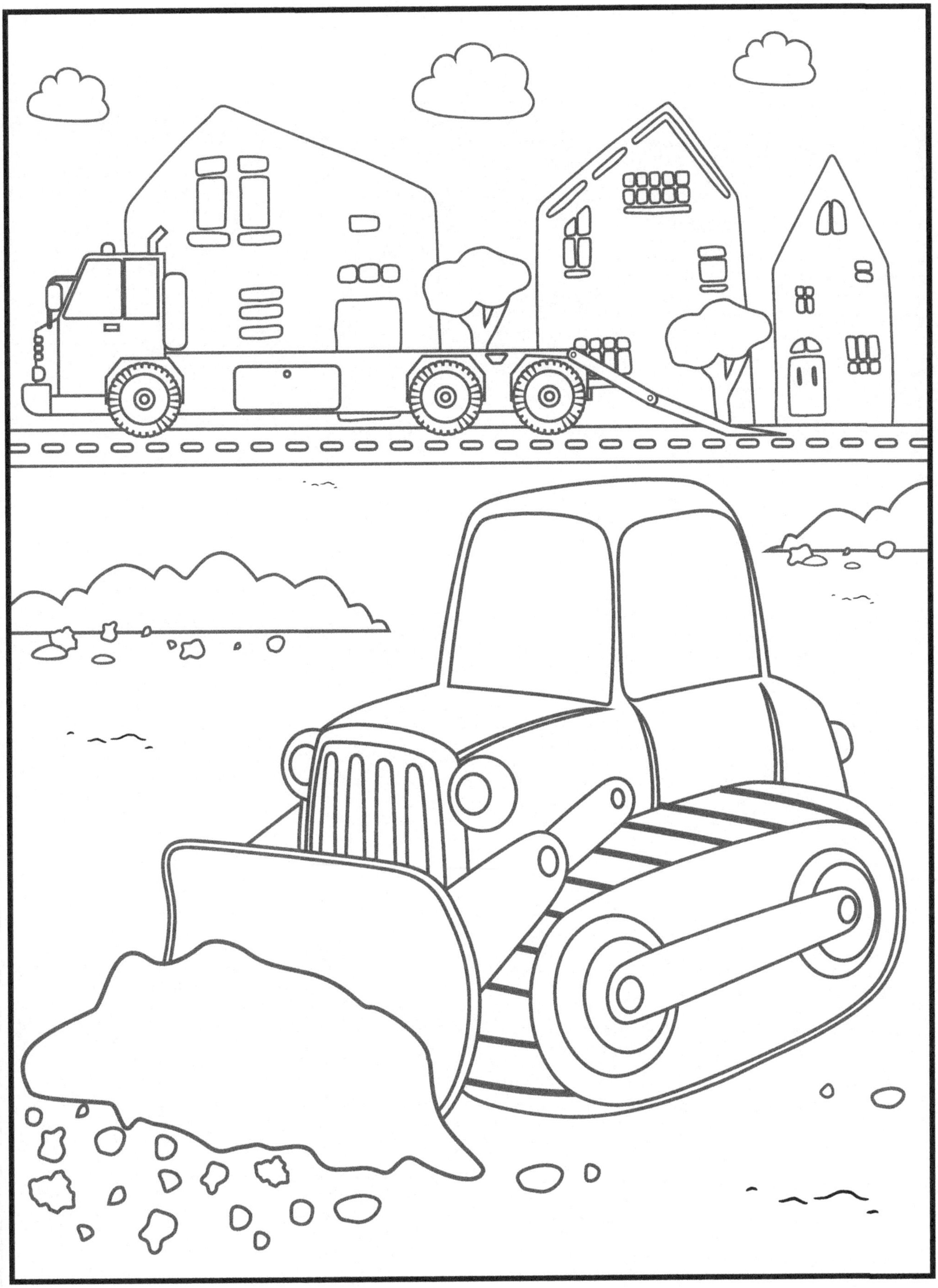

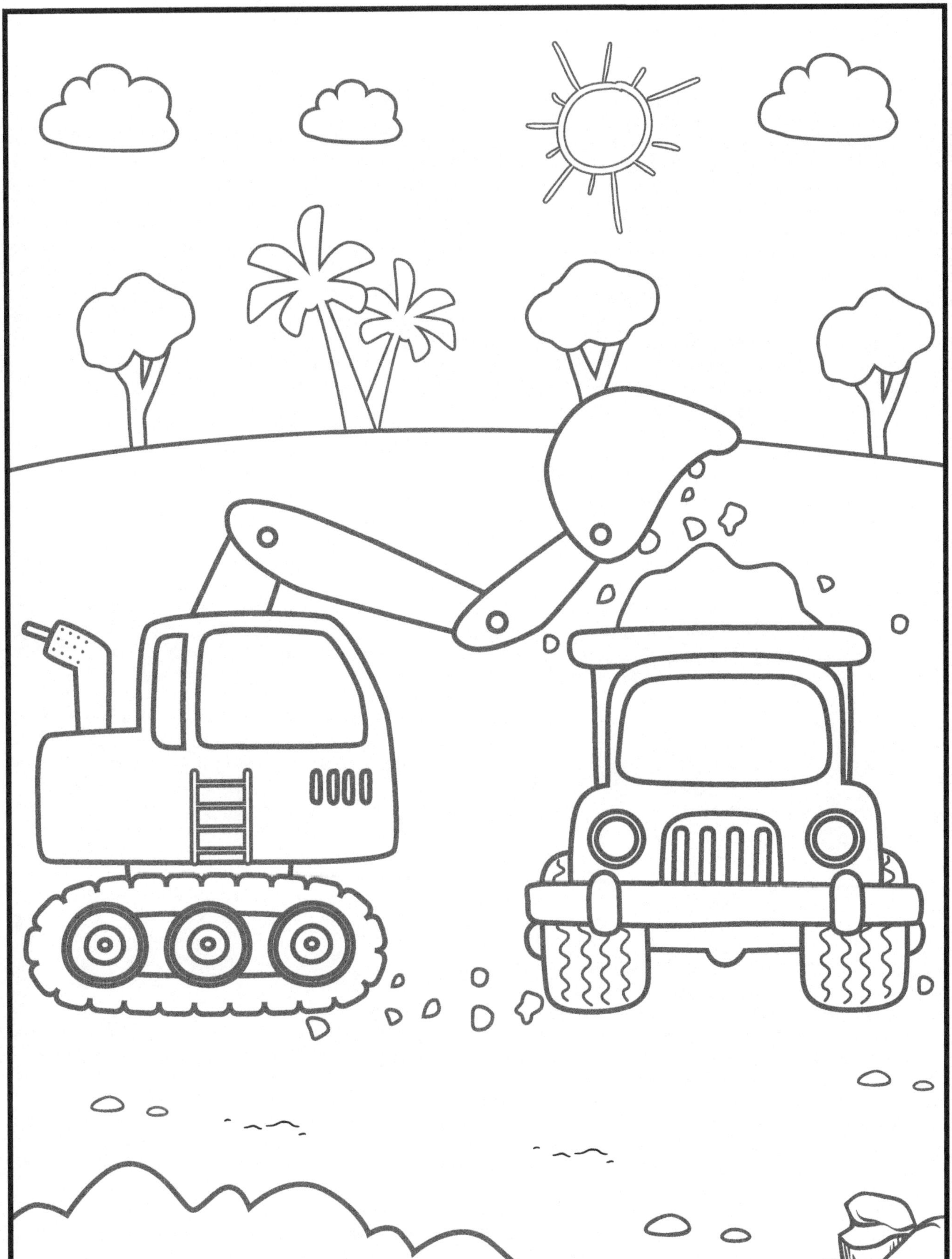

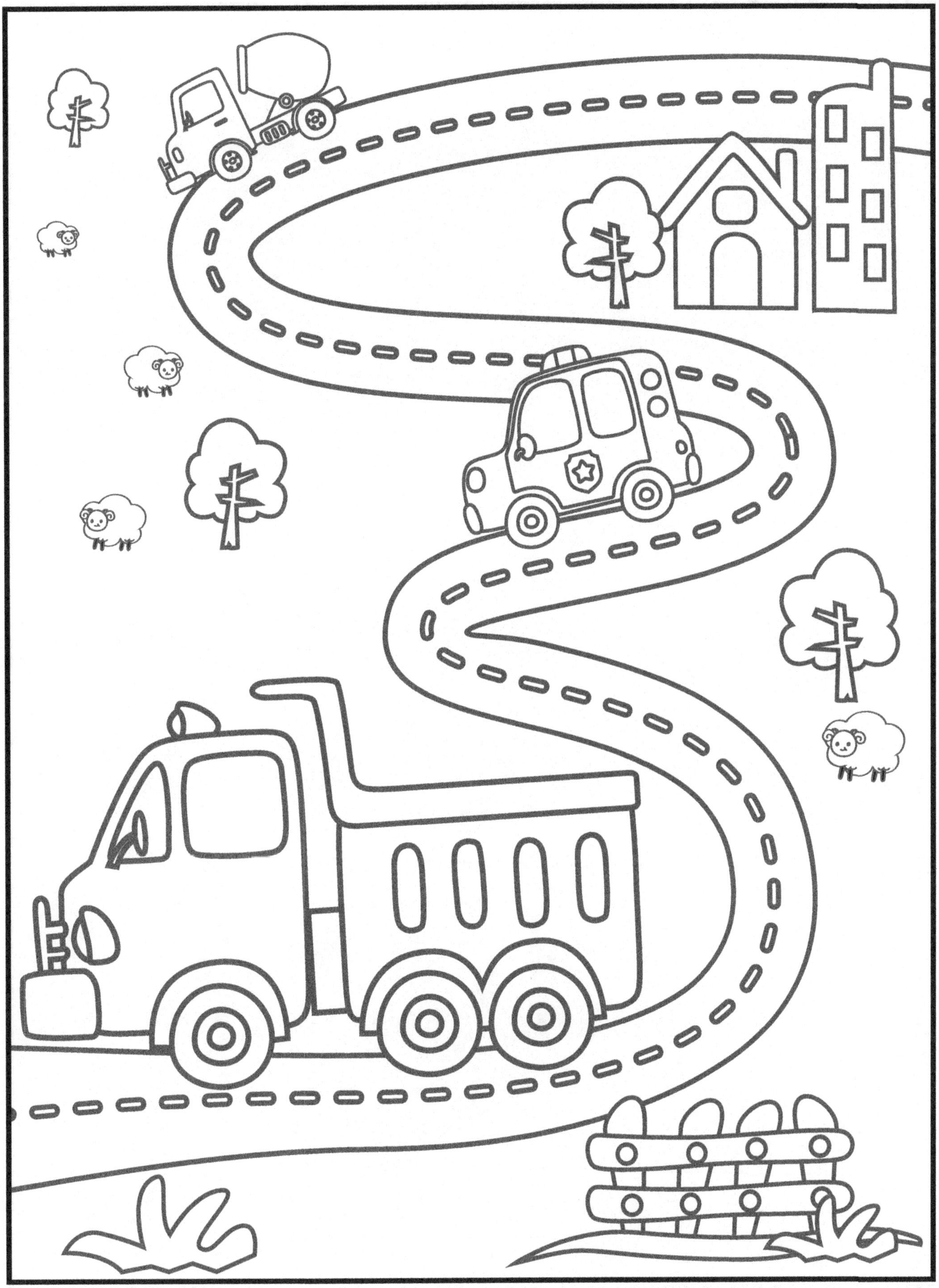

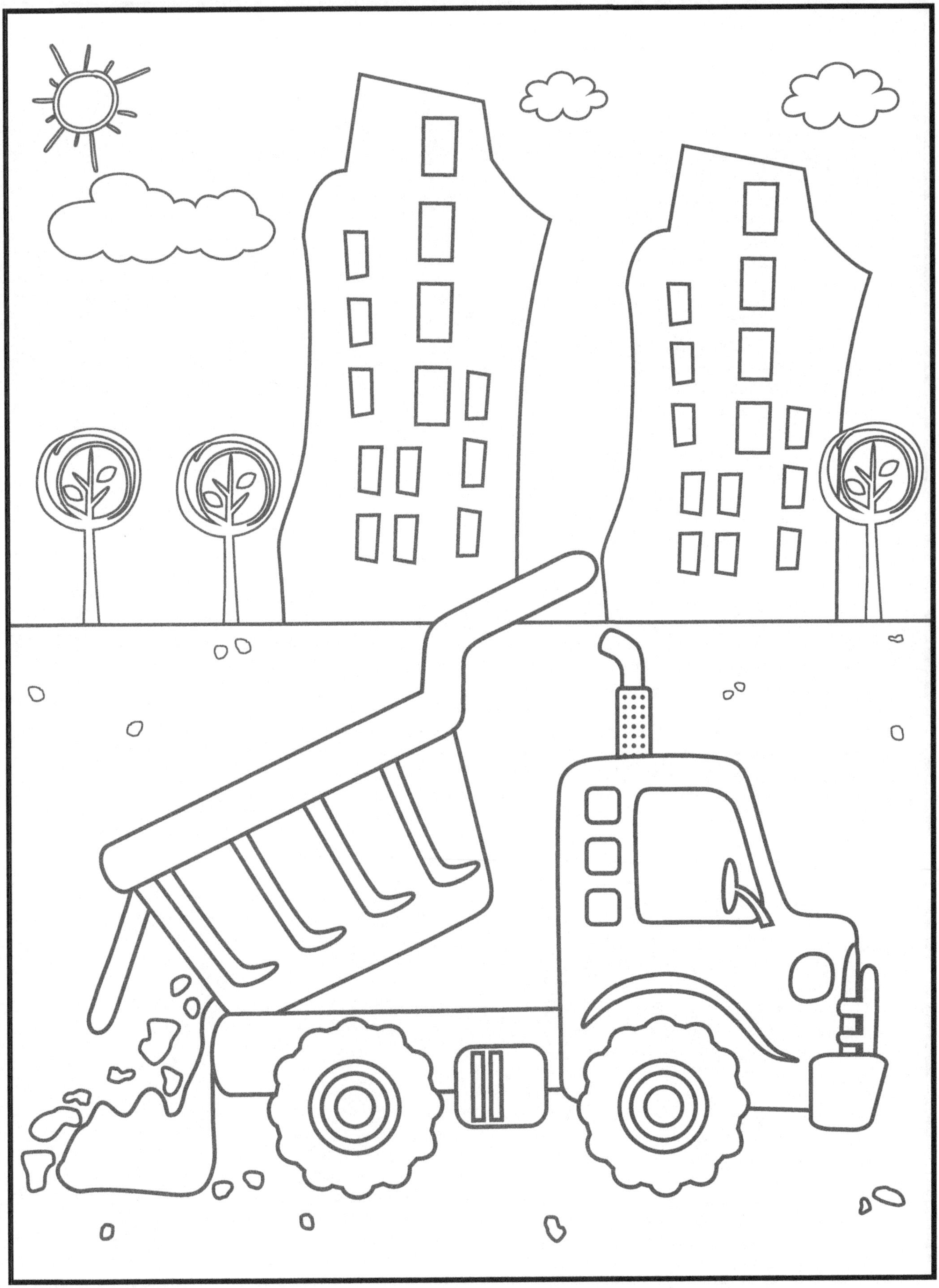

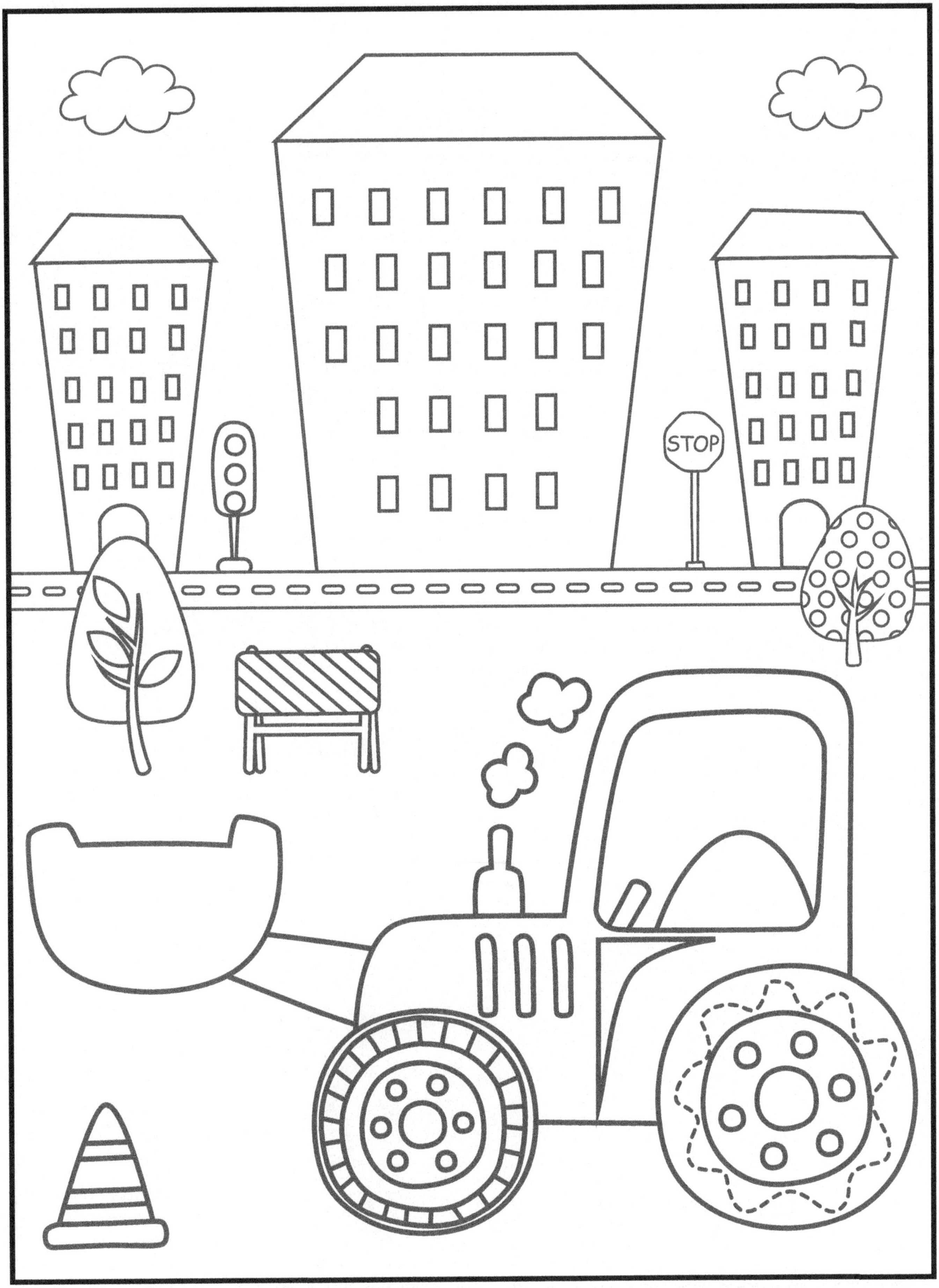
STOP

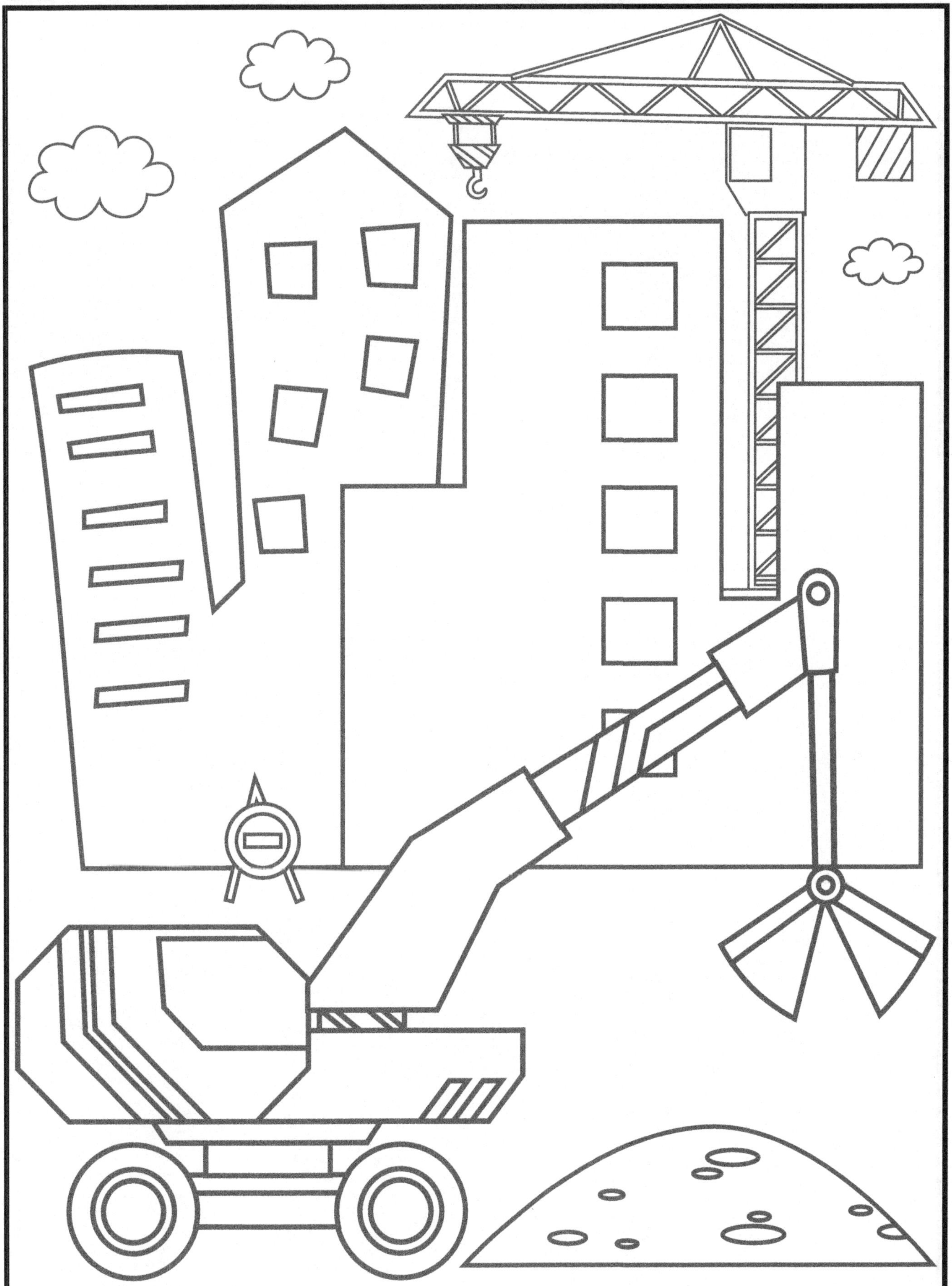

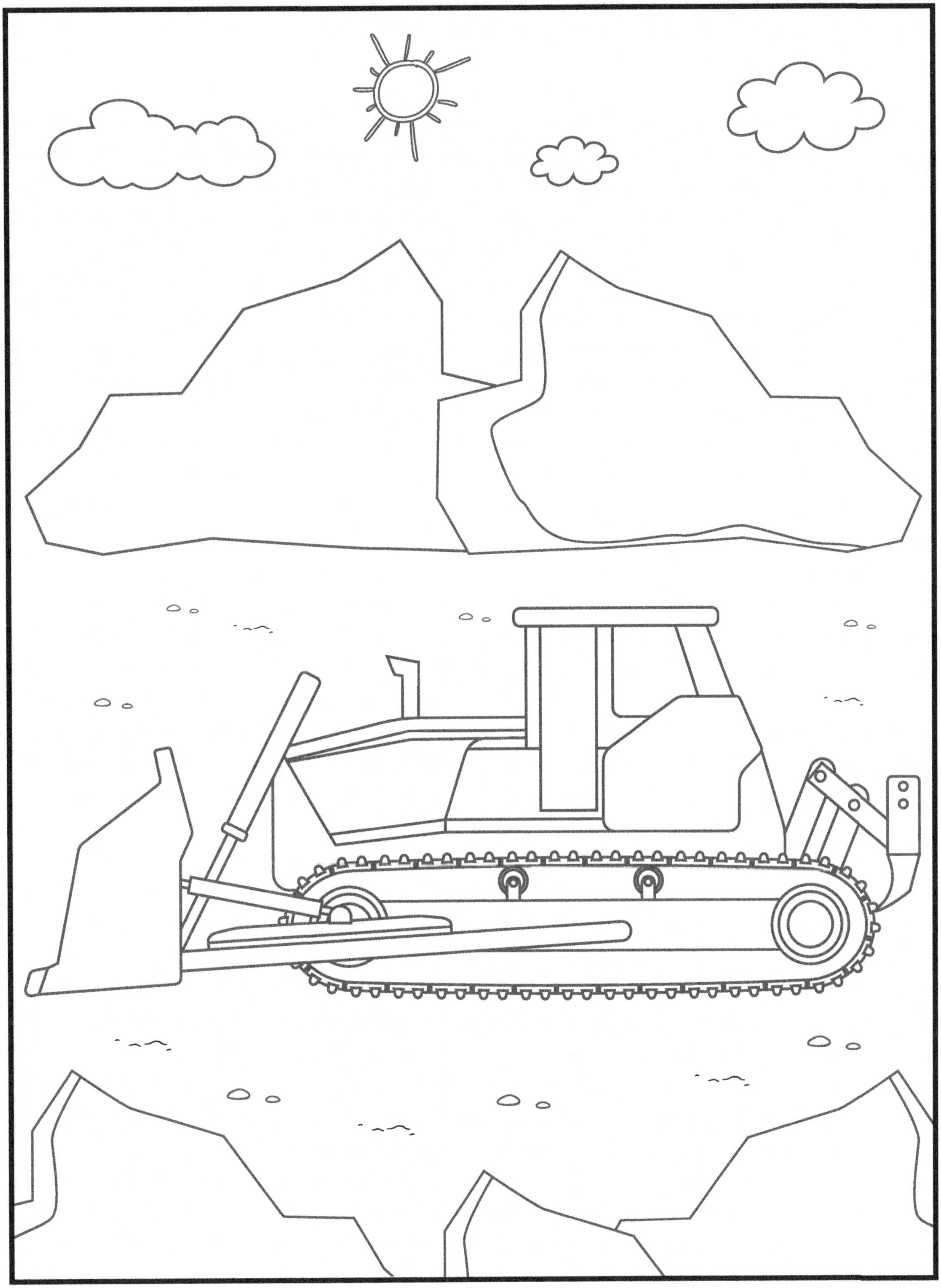

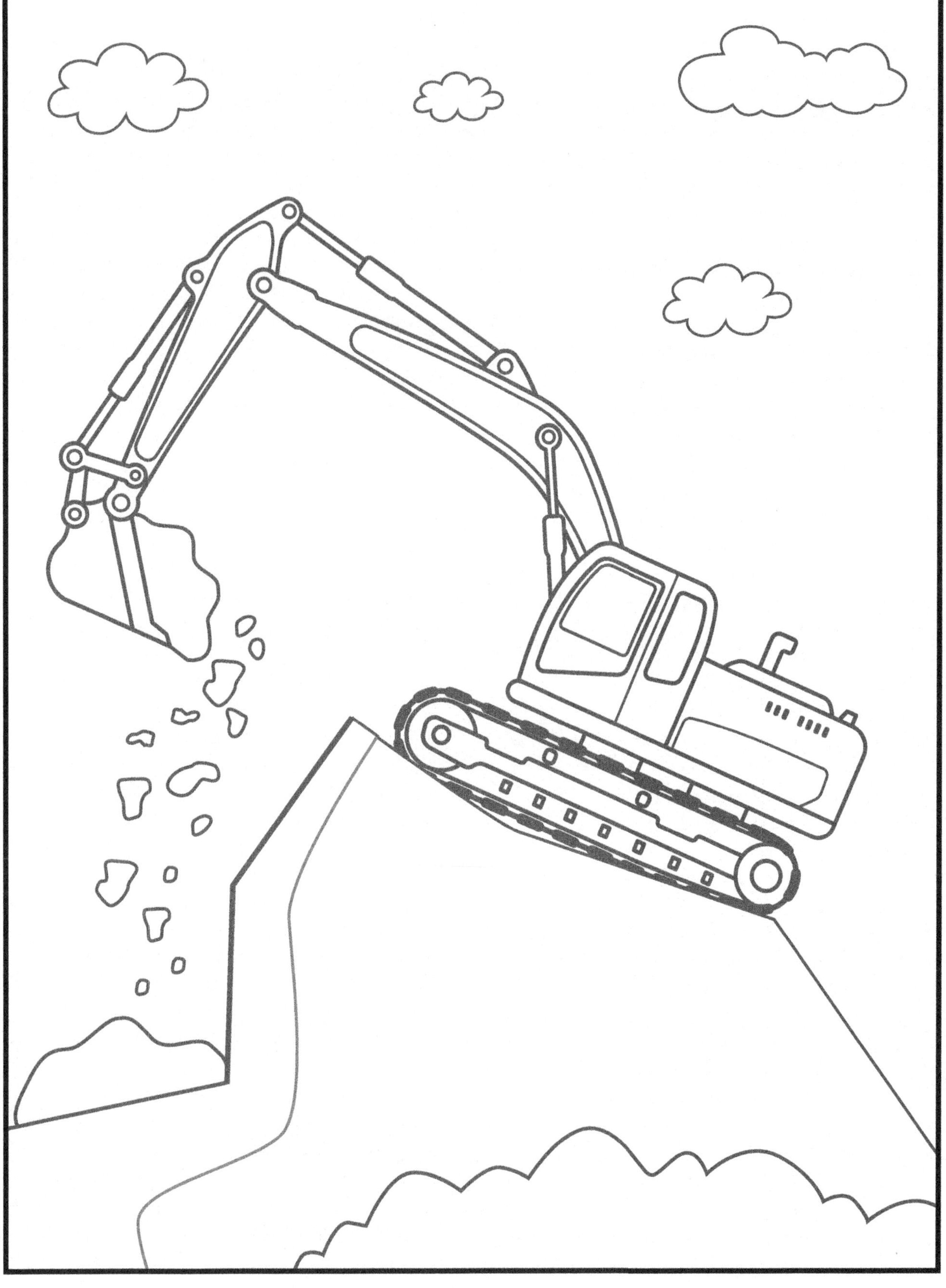

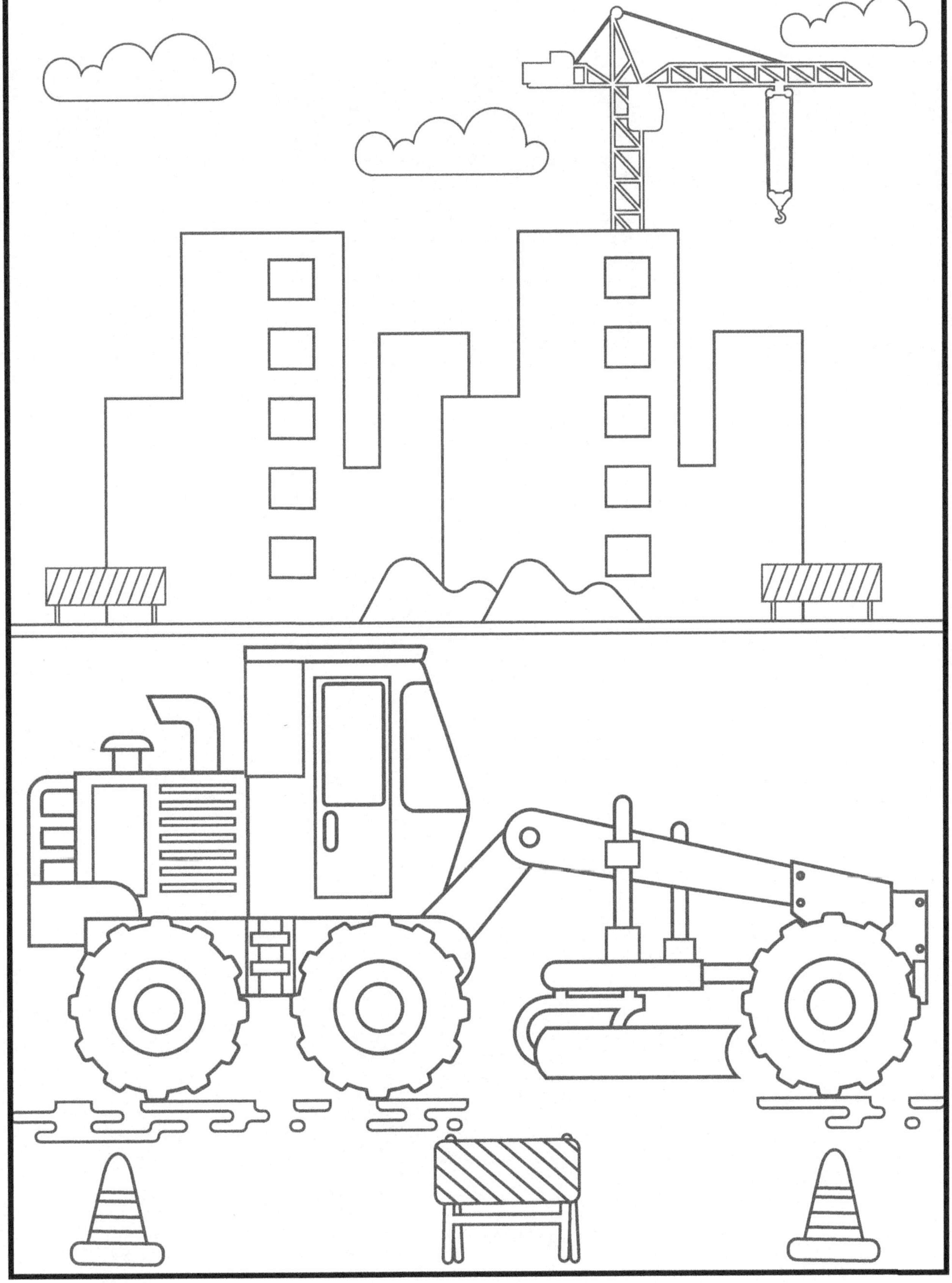

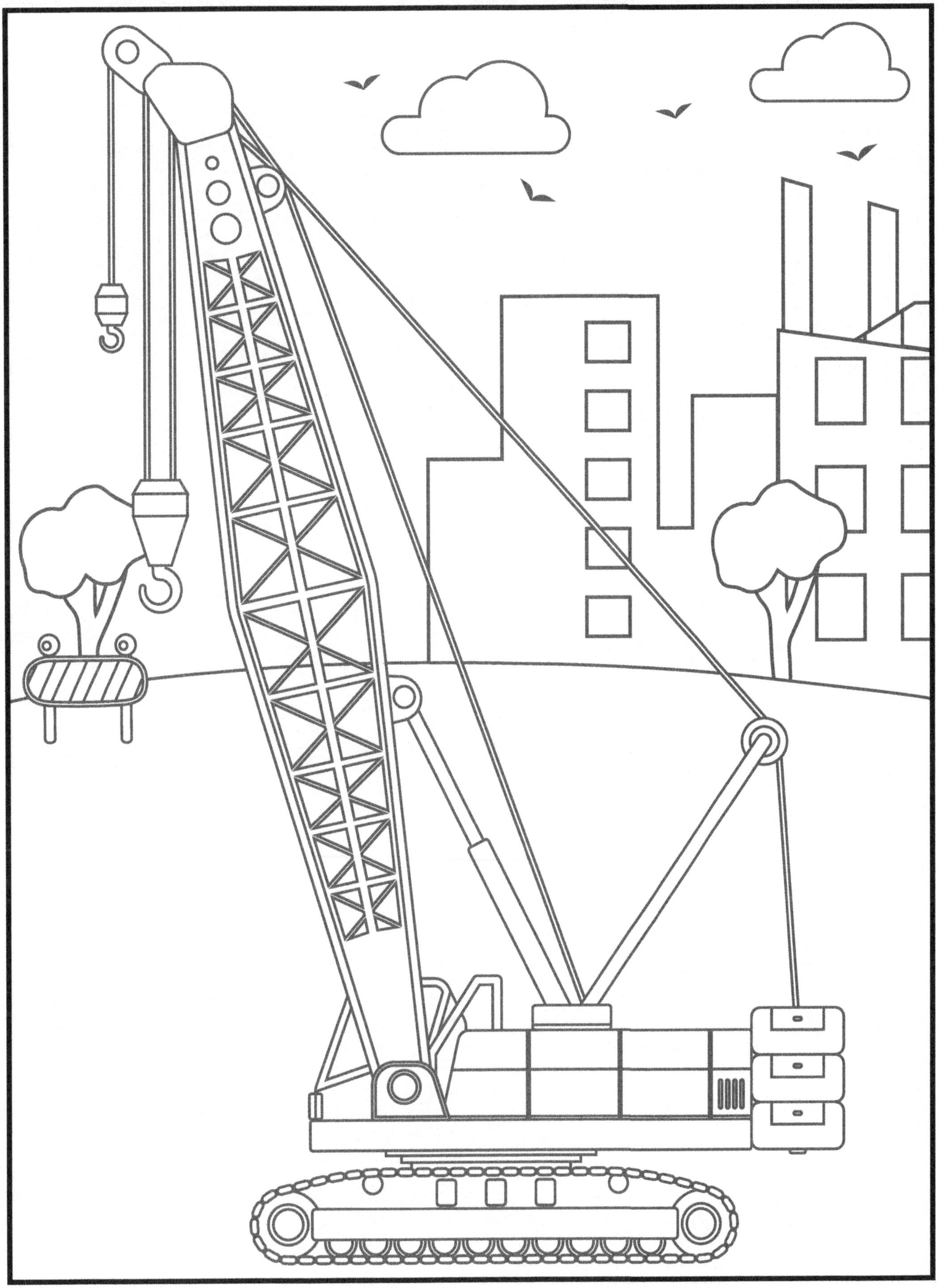

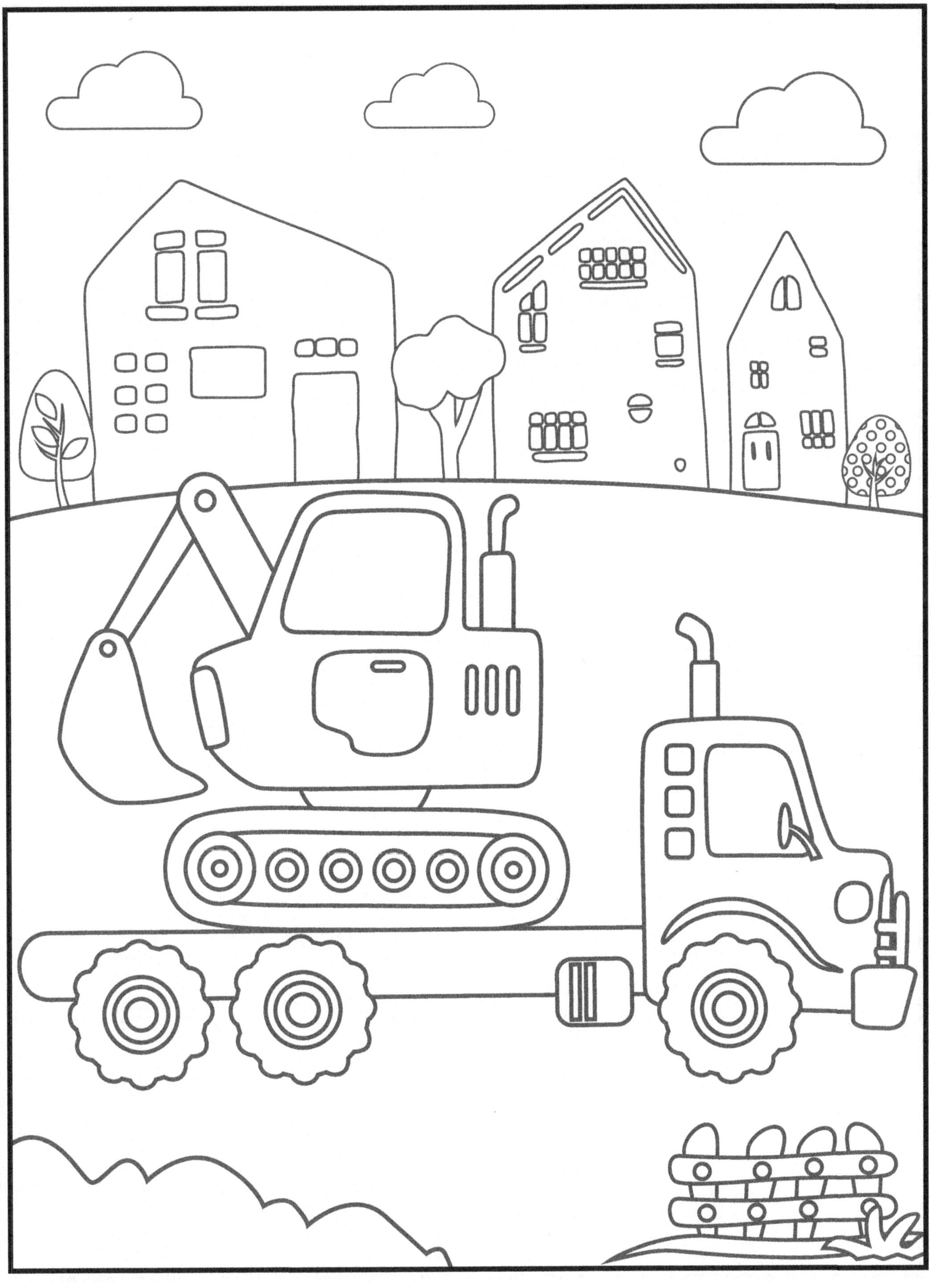

Made in the USA
Las Vegas, NV
14 June 2023

73444449R00046